Investigating Religion

John Bird

Published by Collins Educational
An imprint of HarperCollins*Publishers*
77–85 Fulham Palace Road
Hammersmith, London W6 8JB

The HarperCollins website address is
www.**fire**and**water**.com

www.**Collins**Education.com
On-line Support for Schools and Colleges

First published in 1999
Reprinted 1999, 2001

© HarperCollins*Publishers* Ltd 1999

ISBN 0–00–327508–6

John Bird asserts the moral right to be identified as the author of this work.
A catalogue record for this book is available from the British Library.

Commissioned by Emma Dunlop
Cover design by Derek Lee
Typesetting by Derek Lee
Cartoons by Martin Shovel
Edited by Brigitte Lee and Jack Messenger
Project managed by Kay Wright
Production by Emma Lloyd-Jones
Printed and bound by Scotprint

Contents

Acknowledgements

The author and publisher would like to thank the following individuals and organizations for permission to reproduce material:

Steve Allen, p. 125
Ashgate Publishing Limited, p. 35 (bottom)
James Curley, p. 118
Patricia Briggs, pp. 165, 170
Michael J Browne, p. 14
Cambridge University Press, p. 157
Christian Research, pp. 30, 31, 35
Christian Resources Exhibition, p. 173
The First Church of Christ, Scientist, p. 133
The *Daily Telegraph*, p. 90 (top)
Mary Evans Picture Library, p. 153
The *Guardian* pp. 32, 58, 59, 64, 75 (top), 76, 90 (bottom), 100, 104, 108, 119, 120, 121, 122, 137, 138, 141, 142, 168, 175
Emma Lloyd-Jones, pp. 135 (bottom right), 149, 164
Greenpeace, p. 67
HarperCollins*Publishers* Ltd., pp. 48, 73, 117
Holy Trinity Brompton, p. 110
The Methodist Church, p. 156
The *Observer*, p. 79, 91
Office for National Statistics © Crown copyright, pp. 113, 36, 38, 39
'PA' News Photo Library, pp. 13 (top) John Giles, 52, 102, 104, 127 (David Jones)
Peter Sanders Photography, p. 159
QA Photos/NMEC, p. 171
© Times Newspapers Limited, pp. 49 and 143 (Christopher Morgan), 61, 83 (Rajeev Syal and Cherry Norton), 171 (Nicholas Hellen)
© Times Supplements Limited, pp. 11, 169
Topham Picturepoint, 13 (bottom), 18 (both – bottom, Simone B Leal Ferreira) 46, 150, 151)
Walking Camera, Alex Keene, pp. 34, 40, 79, 135 (except bottom right), 136
Les Wright, p. 29
Kay Wright, pp. 3, 38, 66, 70, 79, 80, 110, 121, 124, 143, 144, 173

While every effort has been made to contact copyright holders, the publishers would be pleased to hear from any copyright holders who have been overlooked.

Introduction: the sociology of religion

Key terms	Key thinkers
Universalization	Emile Durkheim
Western/non-Western	Sigmund Freud
Multiculturalism	Karl Marx
Church	Georg Simmel
Gender	Max Weber
Modernity	
Secularization	

Introduction

What is the sociology of religion and what do sociologists of religion actually study? In a way it is easier to describe what the sociology of religion is *not*. For instance, sociologists of religion do *not* study the truth or validity of religious beliefs; nor do they set out to prove or disprove the doctrines of particular religions. Sociologists of religion may or may not have religious beliefs of their own; they may be favourably or unfavourably disposed towards religion. Whatever their personal beliefs, these should not affect the way sociologists work; nor should they influence their conclusions.

As a student of the sociology of religion, you too may be a believer or non-believer, you may have positive or negative feelings about religion, or you may simply be indifferent about religious belief. Whatever your point of view, you must try to develop what Mills (1963) calls a *sociological imagination* when you study religion. Among other things, this means putting your personal beliefs to one side in order to study the phenomena you wish to investigate. It is vital to remember that it is not the job of the sociologist to agree or disagree about the truth or falsity of religious belief.

So what *do* sociologists of religion actually study? Sociologists of religion are interested primarily in:

● *what* people believe – the *content* of their religious beliefs;

● *why* people believe – the *reasons* for their religious beliefs;

● the *social organization* of religion – the groups in which people *practise* their religion;

● the role of religious beliefs, practices and organizations in the *wider society*.

In short, sociologists are interested in the *social organization and social consequences of religious belief and practice.*

Explanations and definitions

Any book about the sociology of religion has to start with some important explanations and definitions. The discipline of sociology – not just the sociology of religion, but sociology as a whole – was established largely by people who lived and worked in the late nineteenth and early twentieth centuries: thinkers such as Durkheim, Freud, Marx, Simmel and Weber. They were usually male and most of them lived in Europe. These founders of sociology continue to have an enormous influence on contemporary sociology, including the sociology of religion. In many ways, they set the sociological agenda: that agenda proved to be relevant for over a hundred years and may well continue to be so for another hundred.

Universalizing the familiar

However, because sociology began in Europe (and later, North America) many sociologists tended from the outset to confine their investigations to European and North American societies. The sociological findings of these investigations were then applied – or assumed to apply – rather generally to all sorts of other societies. In the sociology of religion, for example, conclusions arrived at by studying the social organization and social consequences of Christian religions in Europe were **universalized**: that is, they were extended so as to apply to all religions, everywhere. Only rarely did early sociologists actually investigate religions in other parts of the world (usually by means of secondary sources, not from direct investigation); but they also universalized their findings, even though the societies and religions they examined differed enormously.

Sociologists of religion still have to cope with the consequences of this historical bias towards Christianity, Europe and North America. In the past (and sometimes in the present) sociologists have equated Christianity with the familiar and equated other religions with the unfamiliar and exotic. For example, this book would be guilty of favouring Christianity above other religions if it assumed readers were familiar with its beliefs and practices, but thought it necessary to explain the beliefs and practices of other religions. For many sociology students the exact opposite is the case.

Similarly, as you will see throughout this book, much of the statistical data available to sociologists of religion are about Christianity (for example, church membership). It is tempting to analyse these data and assume that one's findings also apply to other religions. This temptation should be resisted; we need to be very careful in our use of such data and very clear about what they actually tell us, particularly when we wish to draw conclusions about religion in general.

East is East and West is West?

The historical bias towards European and North American societies is also apparent in the use of such terms as 'Western' and 'non-Western', the meanings of which have become increasingly uncertain. A hundred or more years ago, 'Western' really did mean the West (i.e. Europe and North America), but even then it was a convenient label for those few powerful industrialized nations – such as Britain – that had colonies around the world. Over time, as more and more nations industrialized and became as 'modern' (see p. 16) as the West, 'Western' and 'non-Western' gradually lost much of their geographical specificity. Nowadays, 'Western' is more a label for all those industrialized nation-states – no matter where they are in the world – whose capitalist- and growth-oriented economies and political systems are interconnected. Japan, for example, is geographically situated in the East (at least it is on British maps!), but its powerful economy and complex social organization are often described as 'Western'. The spread of 'Western-style' political and economic arrangements around the world is part of what is meant by the term 'globalization' (see Chapter 5, pp. 57–8).

Similarly, world religions used to be categorized as Western and non-Western, which usually meant that European and North American Christian religions were prioritized. This categorization has lost its relevance in countries like Britain, where religious beliefs and traditions have diversified as society has become **multicultural**. Patterns of migration over the last fifty years have led to the growth of such world religions as Buddhism, Hinduism, Islam and Sikhism in Britain, religions once thought of as specifically 'Eastern'. In addition, modern communications technologies mean that many people have access to a much wider variety of religious beliefs.

Multiculturalism

Many of the economic and social processes in modern societies (see p. 16) tend to **universalize** a mainstream culture from which minority cultures are largely excluded. The mass media (especially television), for example, may provide access to a wide variety of religious beliefs, but much advertising and programming pulls in the opposite direction by focusing on a narrow range of images and lifestyles. Unless they are specifically targeted by advertisers, women and people from ethnic minority groups are under-represented, and when they *are* shown it is often as stereotypes. The languages and cultural artefacts of ethnic minority groups are almost wholly ignored. ▶

The educational system often ignores or stereotypes minority cultures.

Multiculturalism seeks to resist this cultural unification by celebrating and promoting cultural variety and pluralism.

All this can be very confusing, so this book tries very hard not to describe religions in terms of geography. Where this cannot be avoided, try to bear in mind the difficulties and limitations that these historical biases have introduced.

What do we mean by 'church'?

As we have seen, the sociology of religion was established and developed largely in the context of Christianity as practised in Europe and North America. This had an enormous influence on sociological definitions of religion and the labels and terms used by sociologists of religion. For example, sociological definitions of religion have included reference to a single God, whereas many world religions have many gods, or no gods at all. Confusingly for students of sociology today, discussions about religious organization still often use the terms *churches* and *denominations*, words that in everyday use are normally applied specifically to Christianity. Although the *sociological* meanings of 'church' and 'denomination' are not the same as their everyday meanings, these words still seem inappropriate and can be very confusing when applied to religions other than Christianity.

This book tries to avoid using such terms unless absolutely necessary or when they refer unambiguously to Christianity. Instead of 'church' (= building), for example, we use 'place of worship'; instead of 'going to church' we use 'attend worship'. Instead of 'church' (= religious group) we use 'religious organization' or 'religion'.

There are many types of religious organization and many different places of worship. We must always beware of the dangers of applying sociological terms cross-culturally and in inappropriate contexts.

Gender

Over the last thirty years or so sociologists have become much more aware of the importance of **gender** (see Chapter 9). At the same time that early sociology oriented itself towards Europe and North America, it also tended to focus on men rather than women. As we have seen, those thinkers traditionally regarded as the founders of sociology were all men. Sociology, like many other academic disciplines, has had to acknowledge that for most of its history it has been dominated by male practitioners. Many of these practitioners have presumed that social divisions based on gender and ethnicity are in some way 'natural'. In the sociology of religion, this has meant that many of the conclusions based on the study of Christian religions in

Europe and North America – religions in which men have most power and authority – also embody a gender bias towards men.

What is modernity?

It is important to remember that sociology as a whole developed in Europe and North America at a time of rapid industrialization and urbanization. The industrial revolutions which took place – first in Britain, then later in other European countries and North America – led to profound changes in those societies. They became far more complex in their social organization and the pace of social change increased dramatically. Sociologists call these kinds of societies *modern* societies. Modern societies now exist throughout the world. They tend to be large, complex, industrialized and mostly urban; they are often highly economically productive, with varying levels of economic and other forms of inequality; some are democratic, others are not; they often contain a wide range of different cultures and belief systems.

Sociology, therefore, began in the context of **modernity** and it was the religion of *modern* societies that was the primary focus of interest for sociologists. The central question for sociologists of religion was:

● What is the nature and role of religion in the modern world?

This question was asked by just about all the founders of sociology. They argued that religion claims to *explain* such things as the reasons for inequality, poverty and disease and, in doing so, often provides *justifications* for these states of affairs. In so doing religions explain and justify how society is organized, often serving to maintain *social order* and *social solidarity* (see Chapter 2, pp. 9–12).

Sociological explanations of religion

If religious people are asked why they practise their religion, they may say it is because they have faith, or because they believe; they may also say they are religious because their faith will guarantee them salvation. Sociologists of religion explain religious belief and practice in other terms. For example, Durkheim (and subsequently many other sociologists) explains how religion can celebrate and maintain social rules. These two kinds of explanation of religious belief and practice – the *personal* explanation given by the believer and the *sociological* explanation – may or may not be mutually exclusive: it is possible for both to be true (or false!). Whatever their studies lead them to conclude, most sociologists agree that sociological investigation often reveals other reasons for religious belief and practice, reasons which most believers would not be able to identify. Sociologically speaking, therefore, the practice of religion is a complex activity.

The founders of sociology were also generally agreed that religion declines as society becomes more modern. Later sociologists have refined the sociological analysis of religion, but they also tend to agree that religion is less important than it was in *premodern* societies (i.e. before the onset of modernity). Sociologists call this decline in the importance of religion **secularization** (see Chapters 6 and 7).

About this book

The chapters that follow concentrate on three broad questions:

● What are the social roles and consequences of religious belief and practice?

● How is religion socially organized?

● What has happened to religion in the modern world?

There is no one answer to any of these questions. As Andrew Greeley suggests, the search for such an answer is futile:

> The relationship between religion and society has been hotly debated in the literature of the sociology of religion. Much of the heat has not generated light, mostly because the combatants persisted in searching for a single model that would explain the relationships between religion and society at all times and in all places.

> (Greeley 1982, p. 131)

Chapter 2 looks at how sociologists have sought to define religion. Definitions have tended to be of two kinds:

● *functional* definitions state what religion *does*;

● *substantive* definitions state what religion *is*.

We will see that these issues of definition are very important, for example, in assessing how religious people are.

Chapter 3 links issues of definition to how we *measure* religious belief and practice; that is, what sociologists call *religiosity*. Sociologists have attempted to measure religious *practice* – whether people attend worship, for example – and religious *belief*. Neither of these is easy to measure, nor are available data easy to interpret.

Chapter 4 looks at how religion is organized; that is, the social institutions within which people practise and believe. The chapter discusses a basic sociological classification of religious organizations – church, denomination, sect and cult – and examines, for example, how religious sects can evolve into churches or denominations.

Chapter 5 extends the sociological analysis of religious organization by looking at what sociologists have called new religious movements (NRMs) and new age movements (NAMs). NRMs developed in the 1970s and resemble sects; NAMs were common in the 1980s and 1990s and form part of what some sociologists call a cultic milieu (a label that indicates the extent to which the beliefs, practices and products of such organizations have penetrated the wider society).

Chapters 6 and 7 discuss the sociological debate about the process of secularization. Not all sociologists accept the idea that religion has declined, even though there is evidence, for example, that membership of many Christian churches is falling.

Chapter 8 focuses on the diversity of religions in Britain and the importance of religious practice and belief for people from ethnic minority groups.

Chapter 9 investigates the links between religion and other social divisions, especially gender. It describes the social significance of religion for women and takes up part of the debate about the role of women clergy.

Chapter 10 looks at the relationships that sociologists have identified between religion and processes of social change. It concentrates especially on those relationships identified by Weber (and subsequent sociologists and historians) between religion and the development of modern, capitalist societies. The chapter includes a case study on the Islamic Revolution in Iran.

Chapter 11 discusses the idea of the *postmodern* society and its significance for the sociological study of religion; in particular, the importance of mass communication technologies and the availability of an increasingly diverse range of belief systems.

Each chapter concludes with sample examination questions and a list of further reading. Where appropriate, coursework suggestions and data response questions are also included.

References and further reading

Greeley, A. (1982) *Religion: A Secular Theory*, New York: Free Press.

Mills, C.W. (1963) *The Sociological Imagination*, Harmondsworth: Penguin.

2 Defining religion

Key terms	Key thinkers
The sacred	Emile Durkheim
Manifest function	Karl Marx
Latent function	Max Weber
Social solidarity	Sigmund Freud
Theodicy	Georg Simmel
Function/functionalism	Clifford Geertz
Religious surrogates	Milton Yinger
Religious belief	Peter Berger
Religious practice	
Modernity	
Ideology	

Introduction

In this chapter, we will look at how sociologists have defined religion and at how useful such definitions are. In particular, we will look at functional definitions – what religion *does* – and substantive ones – what religion *is*. As we saw in Chapter 1, the founders of sociology all studied religion and had views on how it should be defined and what role religion plays in society. Later sociologists have used and developed these definitions. In addition, this chapter will look at some of the studies of religion carried out by social anthropologists in small-scale, premodern societies; these studies have played an important part in how sociologists look at religion in the modern and postmodern worlds.

> *Application activity*
>
> Thus far, no one has been able to offer a definition of religion that is both precise and sufficiently comprehensive.
>
> (Simmel 1997, p. 101)
>
> *Try to do what Simmel says no one has managed:*
>
> *1 define religion, and*
> *2 compare your definition with those of others in your group.*
>
> *What do your definitions have in common?*
> *How do they differ?*

Why do we need a definition of religion?

What do we mean by a definition?

This may seem like a rather odd question and you may think that it is obvious what a definition is. However, think about defining a table. There are two sorts of definition we could put forward. One would start by deciding what are the essential features of an everyday item such as a table – legs, flat top, legs that are level and so on. The other would take a number of examples of tables and then decide what they all had in common. The first way of defining can lead to all sorts of problems – do tables have to have four legs and a flat top? The second avoids those issues and would allow for tables with any number of legs and either flat or uneven tops. As we will see, definitions of religion often pose problems when the first sort of definition is attempted. Saying that religion is about the supernatural, for example, simply leaves us with another issue of definition: that is, what do we mean by the supernatural? The second approach to definition – take examples of all the things people say are religions and then work out what they have in common – is probably more productive.

A definition of religion is a useful starting point for the sociologist as a way of distinguishing one aspect of social life from another – if we are going to study religion, we need to have some idea of what is and what is not a religion! Other areas of the sociology courses many of you are studying also include issues of definition – definitions of the family or social class, for example. However, precise definitions, as the quotation from Simmel indicates, are difficult to provide.

Defining religion

Most sociologists have attempted to define religion by making lists of essential features, either of what religion *is* or what it *does*.

Functional definitions of religion

Any definition which says, for example, that religion unites people into communities, that it explains why people die, are poor or become ill, is a **functional** definition. The implication here is that religion is an important part of society. Not only do people need answers to important questions – for example, 'Why is my group experiencing oppression?' – but also the answers to those questions have an important role to play in maintaining society as it is. There is a further implication of the idea that religion is functionally important: that a society without religion, or without institutions that fulfil the functions of religion, is unlikely to prosper.

Functionalism

Functional definitions of religion are related to a particular theoretical perspective in sociology called **functionalism**. A number of sociologists (Parsons 1951; Merton 1957) and social anthropologists (Malinowski 1922; Evans-Pritchard 1965; Gluckman 1956) have argued that social institutions and belief systems have the function of maintaining society. Society is orderly and social life ➤

predictable *because* institutions and beliefs perform a range of essential functions. In Gluckman's case, social conflict itself is seen as functional.

There are two major problems with such a view. First, how do we explain social change? If everything, including social conflict, maintains the existing social structure, then it is difficult to see how we could explain how structures *change*. Unless social change happens because of some external factor – for example, the arrival of a new social group from outside – it is difficult to see how change can happen.

Second, how do we deal with things that do *not* appear to maintain social order? To take an example, many people who are not sociologists claim that crime is *dysfunctional*; that is, it causes major social problems and may indicate that society itself is under some kind of threat. However, some functionalist sociologists claim, on the contrary, that even crime can be functional. This leaves us with a major problem: is any social behaviour dysfunctional?

Substantive definitions of religion

Any definition which says that religion is, for example, a belief in God or attending a religious service, is a **substantive** one. Substantive definitions try to identify the key features of religion: that it involves a belief in God or the supernatural, for example.

Both of these ways of defining religion allow us to decide, as sociologists, what is and what is not a religion, although, as we will see again and again throughout this book, issues of definition are never finally resolved and there are constant disagreements over how useful particular definitions are. Here are three examples of problems of definition.

- If a functional definition states, for example, that religion explains why people die, does that mean that any institution which explains death is a religious one?

- If, as many functionalists claim, religion deals with 'ultimate problems', how do we decide what these are? Do the same ultimate problems exist in all societies?

- If we define religion substantively and say that it is about a belief in God, for example, can a belief system which does not contain an idea of God count as a religious one?

A Godless creed

RELIGION without God – isn't that a contradiction in terms? Not to a growing number of Britons, it seems. Last month, a MORI poll reported that the majority of Britons do not believe in God – only 43 per cent of those surveyed ticked the box 'I believe that God exists'. Yet a respectable 67 per cent of MORI respondents believe themselves 'to be religious', while 79 per cent believe there is an afterlife. 'This is surely the paradox of our time,' says Robert Ashby, director of the British Humanist Association, which commissioned the poll – 'a growing sense of religiosity without gods'.

It is a paradox openly embraced by the 700 or so clergy and lay people in a small but significant movement known as the Sea of Faith network. Most do not believe in God 'out there', in the traditional sense. Rather, they see religion, like art and science, as a human creation. Yet – and this is the interesting bit – you would be hard pressed to find people more deeply committed to religious ideas, rituals and ways of life. The demise of God may not, after all, entail the death of religion.

The network was sparked off by Don Cupitt's prolific writings, and his influential 1984 TV series, *The Sea of Faith*. Cupitt – an Anglican priest, philosopher-theologian and fellow of Emmanuel College, Cambridge – writes of religion after God, religion that consists simply of spirituality and a way of life. God, as a symbol of our highest ideals, becomes the spiritual requirement – the inner demand that we fashion our lives in accordance with this highest ideal.

Source: *Times Higher Education Supplement*,
19 July 1996

Interpretation and application activity

What is the main argument of the Sea of Faith network?

Develop a substantive definition of religion which does not contain a reference to God.

If we take one particular definition of religion – the one provided by Durkheim – we can see how functional and substantive definitions can be combined and how useful that combination can be, despite what we have said above.

> A religion is a unified set of beliefs and practices relative to sacred things, that is to say, things set apart and forbidden – beliefs and practices which unite into one single moral community called a Church – all those who adhere to them.
>
> (Durkheim 1912/1961, p. 47)

The **functional** elements of this definition refer to how religions link people together in communities and provide what Durkheim calls social solidarity. The **substantive** elements refer to religion as being about beliefs and practices which identify some things as sacred. Durkheim's definition has a number of important features.

- *Religion is about beliefs and practices.* For Durkheim, religion combines social practices (for example, attending worship) and beliefs (for example, a belief in

God). According to Durkheim, all social activities have this combination of practices and beliefs; there can be no religion which is simply about beliefs, because beliefs affect how people behave socially. The way people practise their beliefs may change – as we will see in Chapters 3 and 6, fewer people now attend worship regularly – but many people *do* and others practise their religion in their daily lives without seeing the need to attend worship on a regular basis.

● *The sacred is central to religion.* Durkheim makes a distinction between the secular – our everyday lives – and the **sacred**. The sacred is everything that is outside our normal, daily lives and very often includes beliefs in supernatural beings or forces. It is the sacred which makes religion special. Things which are regarded as sacred are dealt with by a religion in a careful, ritualized way. Good examples are the Mass held in Anglican and Roman Catholic churches and the weekly worship at a mosque required by Muslims. For sociologists, the sacredness of the Mass is shown in the way that specialized individuals – priests – organize and lead the ritual; also, the people who attend the Mass do so with a feeling that it *is* sacred and they have to follow a set, recognized pattern of activities.

● *Religions link people together into communities.* This linking into communities arises because people practise their religion together: that is, they practise religious rituals. These rituals have a central role in developing and maintaining **social solidarity**. Participation in religious rituals not only makes people feel a close bond with others in their community, it also helps people to accept social rules; that is the point about the moral community in Durkheim's definition.

Notice how sociological this approach is: whatever worshippers say they are doing – praying to God, confessing their sins – they are *really* involved in a process which has an entirely different function, that of maintaining social solidarity by generating strong feelings of attachment to social rules.

Manifest and latent functions

Robert Merton (1957) argued that social institutions and beliefs function on two levels. There are the **manifest functions** of something – religion helps people to understand disasters and that is what believers say it is for. However, there are also **latent functions** of that belief – religion binds people into social groups that come into conflict with other religious groups. Believers may not be aware of these latent functions, but it is one of the jobs of sociologists to uncover them.

One of the implications of religion binding people into their communities is that it can also divide people from one another; one religious community may see itself as opposed to another.

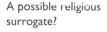

The example of Northern Ireland

Historically, religious divisions have been especially important in Northern Ireland. They have become the ways in which the two major religious groups – Protestant and Roman Catholic – understand their history and their present social situation. People have come to see their employment prospects, how much political influence they have, their education, their whole culture, in religious terms. The dispute over marching by Protestant religious groups indicates also how the territory of towns and cities is divided along religious lines.

The case of Northern Ireland indicates how religious affiliation can at the same time *unite* groups of people and *oppose* those groups to others. The social solidarity of one religious group is, in part, maintained by its opposition to another group.

There are difficulties with Durkheim's approach which indicate some of the problems about providing precise and all-purpose definitions of religion.

First, are all beliefs and practices that maintain social solidarity, religions? At first sight, the answer is 'no'. Voting in a general election maintains the importance of the voting system and indicates people's commitment to democracy, but voting is clearly not a form of religion. However, the answer 'no' raises some serious questions. For example, can we have a society without religion? If so, what performs the function of maintaining social solidarity in such a society? Are there **religious surrogates** (institutions and beliefs that perform the function of religion in maintaining social solidarity), for example, nationalism?

As Lane (1981) points out, people in the Soviet Union visited Lenin's tomb and did so with great reverence. Lenin seemed to be treated as a sacred object, signifying the triumph of communism. As such, visiting his tomb displayed a feature essential, for

A possible religious surrogate?

Durkheim, to religion: that is, the sacred. Therefore, in a society that was expressly anti-religious, religious activities continued to exist. Lane's work also suggests that rituals are important in complex, modern societies.

Durkheim almost gets around this problem of surrogates by arguing that the really important thing about social life is that people come together in groups to do things *collectively*. Some of these things are recognizable religious rituals, but others are not so obviously religious. For Durkheim this hardly matters; as he says:

> The essential thing is that men are assembled, that sentiments are felt in common and expressed in common acts; but the particular nature of these sentiments and acts is something secondary.
>
> (Durkheim 1912/1961, p. 386)

Second, there are problems with the idea of the sacred. When we observe religious worship it is fairly easy to decide what the sacred things are: for Christians, the Cross; for Jews, the sacred book of the Torah, and so on. As Durkheim suggests, anything can be a sacred object as long as people *treat* it as sacred. However, there seem to be more sacred things than just the things that religious people treat as sacred: many nationalists treat the national flag as sacred; many football supporters treat the members of their team as sacred, and so on. Clearly, football is not, for the sociologist, a religion, but some of the awe with which people treat religious objects is found in how supporters treat footballers.

The Art of the Game. Picture courtesy of Michael Browne, artist.

Football and religion

Robert Coles (1975) asks whether it is legitimate for sociologists to regard football as a religious surrogate. Whether or not it is legitimate is less important than the issues that this question raises for definitions of religion. There are certain things about going to a football match that are close to religion as defined by Durkheim: large numbers of people with a common purpose; sacred symbols – shirts, pictures, flags; chanting as a way of celebrating your team and opposing the other team; powerful emotions. Coles does not say that football *is* a surrogate religion, but he does say that many of the social processes going on in football grounds are very like those going on in religious worship.

This tells us something about definitions again. If we use a functionalist definition we are more likely to see things as religions that are not obviously religious; this might include football. If we use a substantive definition we are more likely to deny, for example, that football is a religion.

Evaluation activity

Are the following activities religious or are they religious surrogates?

	Religious		Religious surrogates	
	Yes	*No*	*Yes*	*No*
Going to a funeral	☐	☐	☐	☐
Buying a national flag	☐	☐	☐	☐
Visiting a shopping mall	☐	☐	☐	☐
Reading horoscopes	☐	☐	☐	☐

Give reasons for each of your answers.

The founders of sociology and the sociology of religion

As we saw in Chapter 1, the founders of sociology – in particular, Marx, Weber, Durkheim, Simmel and Freud – all had something to say about religion and all were concerned with the relationships between the sort of world they were describing – what we would now call modernity – and religion.

Modernity and modern societies

Sociology developed in the nineteenth and twentieth centuries in two contexts: the shock of a new type of society and the encounter with small-scale societies in Africa, India, South America and elsewhere. The new type of society that sociologists set out to analyse and explain was seen to be modern, hence the use of the word **modernity**. Although there is no agreed definition of modernity, we can identify the main features of modern societies which make them distinct. For example, the UK has a large population; most people live in cities; the organizations in which many people work are large, complex and bureaucratic; scientific ways of thinking about the world have high status; religion seems to have declined in importance (see Chapters 6 and 7); society is complex, with divisions based upon social class, age, gender, ethnicity and region. All these features are characteristic of modernity. They make modern societies different to small-scale, premodern ones, but different also to what Britain was like in the seventeenth or thirteenth centuries.

We have already looked at what Durkheim argued. We will now briefly look at what the other founders of sociology had to say about defining religion and the social roles of religion.

Karl Marx and the opium of the people

Marx, writing with Friedrich Engels, provided what has become a famous definition of religion:

> Religious distress is at the same time the *expression* of real distress and the *protest* against real distress. Religion is the sigh of the oppressed creature, the

heart of a heartless world, just as it is the spirit of a spiritless situation. It is the *opium* of the people. The abolition of religion as the *illusory* happiness of the people is required for their *real* happiness.

(Marx and Engels 1845/1955, p. 38)

Marx's definition is largely functional because it says what religion *does*: that is, that it provides compensation for the fact that people live lives based on exploitation. That exploitation is itself based on divisions between a social class that owns property and hence controls what people do, and those who do not have that power. For Marx, religion is both a *compensator* and a way in which exploitation is *justified* and *concealed*; religion is, in that sense, an **ideology**.

Ideology

For Marx and Engels, there are two ways in which society is held together. First, people have to work in the jobs they do, for example, in order to earn enough to live. Social order, therefore, partly comes about because of this economic necessity. Second, people believe things that make the way that their society works at the moment seem legitimate. They might, for example, regard large inequalities in power and wealth as acceptable, and a religion might justify such inequalities by promising compensation for them in a future life. This is what Marx and Engels mean by ideology, and they suggest a range of ideologies – religion, nationalism, democracy – and a range of ways in which ideologies are disseminated – books, education and so on.

We can take an example here. A religion might say to people that if they work hard in what God has given them to do – be they a teacher, the prime minister, a gardener or an unemployed person – they will, at some future time, be saved or rewarded. Therefore, for Marx, religion has a double function. It persuades some people to put up with their lack of power and others to see their power as God-given and legitimate. It also justifies the existing way in which society is organized: that is, with some people having power and wealth while others have little or none. This double function leads Marx to take a very negative position concerning religion: if people were aware of their real situation then they would challenge it; for example, they might oppose social inequality politically. As an ideology, religion prevents them from doing this.

Notice that, as Durkheim stated, for the sociologist there is a lot more to religion than what believers say they are doing. Religion has social effects of which believers may be completely unaware.

Sigmund Freud and religion as an illusion

Freud's approach has lots of things in common with that of Marx, but lacks the emphasis on how religion serves to justify and conceal social inequality. The title of Freud's main study of religion indicates what he thinks – it is called 'The Future of an Illusion' (1927/1985). As with Marx, for Freud religion serves to hide things as they really are; it prevents us from seeing the situations we really face. In this sense, science may be seen as superior to religion and to eventually replace it. The work of both Marx and Freud predicts that religion will decline as societies become more modern.

Freud adds something to our understanding of religion which is not there in Marx: religion has a *psychological* function in that it prevents us from acting as adults. It is what Freud calls a *neurosis*, something which allows us to remain childlike in the way we deal with other people. For example, religion allows people to see their social problems as a consequence not of their own actions – which would be a mature adult view – but as a result of something God does. This latter way of looking at the world is what, for Freud, makes religions examples of neurosis and infantilism: religions prevent us from behaving as adults and taking responsibility for our own problems.

Like Marx, Freud sees religion as having negative consequences. If people could get beyond religion, they would be able to find better ways to live their lives: they could come to terms with the problems to which religion provides illusory answers – unhappiness, death, underprivilege and so on. For Marx, and to a lesser extent for Freud, religion holds back social progress.

Max Weber and the problem of theodicy

Weber does not provide a precise definition of religion like the ones given by Durkheim and Marx. For Weber, definitions pose as many problems as they solve and, in this case, may exclude many things that people regard as religion.

What makes Weber's approach sociological is that he says that **religious belief** and **religious practice** are always about the wider society and how people live in that society: this is the case even when religion looks, on the surface, to be referring only to supernatural things. In addition, even though religious beliefs often appear strange to non-believers, they are rational. This leads Weber to suggest that issues of definition are rather unimportant and to provide a very simple idea of what all religions have in common: belief in another world beyond the everyday one. This is the way he puts it:

> To define 'religion', to say what it is, is not possible at the start of a presentation such as this. Definition can be attempted, if at all, only at the conclusion of the study. The essence of religion is not even our [the sociologist's] concern.
>
> (Weber 1922/1968)

Other-worldly or this-worldly: people express their religious beliefs in different ways.

Not only does Weber avoid issues of definition but, unlike Durkheim, Marx and Freud, he bases his approach is also based much more on detailed studies of real religions, including those from a wide range of different societies: Protestantism (Western Europe), Hinduism (India), Buddhism and Taoism (China) and Judaism (Middle East).

Weber classifies these different religions in terms of how they tell people to deal with the wider society. Some are **other-worldly**: if you wish to be truly religious you must withdraw from society, for example by becoming a hermit and living in a cave. Others are **this-worldly**: people should be involved in the wider society, as long as they are religious when they do this – for example by working hard in the job God has given them. Both types of religion contain beliefs in some other world of the supernatural, spirits, gods and the like.

Weber also says things about what religion *does*. All religions deal with what Weber calls the problem of **theodicy**. This is a very simple problem which, for Weber, is something all people in all societies have to deal with, if the societies in which they live are to make sense to them. The problem of theodicy is this: how do people come to see the world, with all its dangers, problems and nastiness, as meaningful? The world religions answer a series of questions that we all face: 'Why am I poor?' 'Why have I or my relatives become ill?' 'Why will I die and when?' The religious context of all this is shown in the following question, which many religious people try to answer: 'If God is good and all powerful, why does he make me/my relatives/my group suffer?'

There are a number of different theodicies. Some religious theodicies argue that the world is divided into two opposed forces, good and evil; things go wrong because evil is temporarily on top. Others argue that suffering is a test of faith in God and that, in consequence, suffering is a means to salvation. Still others argue that God has decided whether we will suffer and whether we will, for example, go to heaven, but that we can never know this. As we will see later, religious theodicies have profound consequences for how society works: religious beliefs and practices affect much more than just religion and religious behaviour. What Weber and most sociologists of religion are interested in, therefore, are the social consequences of religious belief and practice.

Finally, for Weber, there is the idea that religious answers to questions about underprivilege, illness and so on might be more satisfying than less religious ones. For example, knowing that you become ill because God is punishing you or your group may be more satisfying than the scientific explanation that you just happened to catch a virus. The religious explanation provides a cause for the illness and relates that cause to how you and your group live your lives; the scientific explanation often does neither of these things. We will come back to this issue when we discuss secularization in Chapters 6 and 7.

Georg Simmel on religion

As we saw in Chapter 1, Simmel suggests that defining religion is difficult and is not an effective starting point for sociologists. He is much more interested in what religion does and in the fate of religion in a modern society.

In terms of what religion does, Simmel comes close to both Durkheim and Weber. He is convinced that religion has an important role to play in developing and maintaining group solidarity and in integrating individuals into social groups. Much more clearly than Durkheim, Simmel is aware of how this may divide social groups from one another. Religious conviction divides people:

> The awareness of the unity of the social group must develop from a twofold contrast: first, the hostile demarcation from other groups ...
>
> (Simmel 1898/1997, p. 173)

This unity has a strong emotional content, which religious worship increases, and it tends to strengthen in periods of crisis. Simmel suggests, for example, a link between war, patriotism and religiosity:

> In periods of intense patriotism ... the relationship of the individual to his groups acquires a certain fervour and dedication that ... [is] of a religious character; there is also at such times a far more pressing need to invoke divine authority. ... Such situations that are characterized by danger and passionate agitation, where the triumph of a political entity is at stake, lend the individual's subjective response to the situation a religious quality and structure.
>
> (Simmel 1898/1997, pp. 154–5)

The Weberian elements in Simmel's sociology of religion are associated with his views on how religion provides not only group identity, but also structures of meaning for individuals in those groups. Religion deals with ultimate problems – life, death, illness – and does so by reference to something beyond the real world. There is something special about religion:

> When I say 'I believe in God' the assertion means something entirely different from the statement 'I believe ... the moon is uninhabited'.
>
> (Simmel 1898/1997, p. 109)

> Our capacity to have faith in a person or group of people beyond all demonstrable evidence – indeed, in spite of evidence to the contrary – is one of the most stable bonds holding society together.
>
> (Simmel 1898/997, p. 170)

Finally, Simmel has views on religion in modern society. First, religion may be a way out of a major problem with modern societies: the requirement for specialization with a complex division of labour. If modern societies have a major flaw then religion provides a temporary way out, in that very different people – from different social classes, ethnic backgrounds and with different abilities – can share the same religion. Second, religion in the modern world takes a particular form:

> No small number of ... individuals satisfy their religious needs by way of mysticism ... the supernatural objects of religious belief have been excised radically, though without these people's religious impulse having been eliminated as a result.
>
> (Simmel 1898/1997, p. 21)

This mysticism is a form of religion outside traditional religious organizations, a sort of generalized religious feeling. We will see in Chapters 4 and 5 that this idea is close to those forms of religious movement called cults and to the cultic milieu.

Summary: religion for the founders of sociology

We can summarize the views of the founders of sociology in terms of the sorts of definition and the essential features of religion. In addition, we can summarize their views on the social roles of religion, particularly whether they see religion as a conservative force or one that is potentially radical.

	Definition	Essential features	Role of religion
Durkheim	Functional/substantive	Sacred, Community	Conservative
Marx	Functional	None	Conservative
Freud	Functional/substantive	God	Conservative
Weber	None/minimal	Theodicy	Conservative or radical
Simmel	None/minimal	None	Conservative or radical

Functions

It is important to recognize that a sociologist can say that religion performs a certain function – let us say, explain misfortune or death – without being committed to that theoretical perspective called functional**ism**. Weber identified the function of religion as dealing with problems of theodicy – why, if God is good and all powerful, bad things happen. He was not, however, a functionalist: for example, he did not think religion played a part in maintaining the existing structure of society.

Social anthropologists and the sociology of religion

Although Durkheim never did any first-hand research on the social role of religion, his was a study that spent most of the time talking about religion in premodern societies. He then went on to argue that in the modern world religion would decline in significance and other institutions might come to do what religions had traditionally done; these **surrogates** might include nationalism, community and democracy. Social anthropologists (for example, Malinowski (1922); Evans-Pritchard (1965); Radcliffe-Brown (1952)) studied small-scale, premodern societies first hand and were often interested in their religious beliefs and practices.

For example, Malinowski's various studies of the Trobriand Islanders of Melanesia included a book called *Argonauts of the Western Pacific* (1922). He argued that the Trobriand Islanders had many magical beliefs which, although they were different from Western religious beliefs, had similar functions, in that they dealt with uncertainty. Fishing, for example, can be a very dangerous activity. Religious and magical beliefs provide people with the confidence to do something dangerous that is essential to the well-being of society and also link people together for that collective enterprise.

Radcliffe-Brown provided a view of religion which implied that it was a necessary feature of society:

> Any religion is an important or even essential part of the social machinery, as are morality and law, part of the complex system by which human beings are enabled to live together in an orderly arrangement of social relations.
>
> (Radcliffe-Brown 1952, p. 154)

For Radcliffe-Brown, the most important aspects of religion are religious rituals, which do two things: first, they emphasize the importance of society and its rules, and, second, they encourage people to accept those rules. This is, of course, very close to Durkheim's view of how religion operates in small-scale societies, ones that Durkheim described as based on **mechanical solidarity**.

Mechanical and organic solidarity

Durkheim argues that small-scale, premodern societies and large-scale, modern ones work in different ways. In the former, there is little specialization in the roles people perform. The division of labour is simple. In those societies characterized by **mechanical solidarity**, there is likely to be a consensus over values, represented in a common religion. As suggested above (p. 12), for Durkheim, when people practise their religion they are, in effect, worshipping society itself. In modern societies order is based on **organic solidarity**. There is no single values system and what maintains social solidarity is the fact that people *are* interdependent and have to rely on each other for essential tasks to be performed. For example, a teacher is dependent on food producers for food. As we will see, the development of organic solidarity has implications for religion and the process of secularization (see Chapter 6).

It is clear, therefore, that the founders of sociology had important things to say about religion. Although they were writing in the nineteenth and early twentieth centuries, we will see throughout this book that either their views are still relevant or that subsequent sociologists have developed their own approaches to religion by criticizing the founders.

The sociology of religion has become an important area of specialization within sociology. For example, within the professional body of sociologists, the British Sociological Association, there is a study group devoted to the sociology of religion which has its own conferences. We will refer to many of these sociologists later in this book, but it is useful to identify some of the key issues here.

● Whereas Marx and Freud were highly critical of religion, seeing it as an illusion, most sociologists of religion would now reject the idea that it is their role to say whether or not religions are valid. Indeed, some of the most eminent sociologists of religion have, themselves, been believers, but their belief has not led them to argue that sociological approaches to religion should deal with issues of whether or not religions are *true*. David Martin (1967), a British sociologist who wrote, among other things, about the process of secularization, and Peter Berger (1973), who wrote about how religion gives meaning to social life, were both committed believers.

● Most sociologists of religion spend very little time with issues of definition because they accept Weber's arguments that definitions are of very little help for the sociologist's main task, which is to see how religion affects what people do. They emphasize the substantive elements of religion. For example, the work of Bryan

Wilson (1961) on religious sects is concerned with how membership of small religious sects helps or hinders how people fit into the wider society.

- Functionalist sociologists, for example Talcott Parsons (1951), are interested in how religion provides a consensus in what people accept as common, core values. For Parsons, society consists of two types of institution – regulative and cultural – which involve two types of social action – instrumental and expressive. Regulative institutions regulate **behaviour** and cultural institutions support significant **social values**. Religions are, therefore, cultural institutions for Parsons and are based on expressive action, although, of course, they may have regulative functions. These ideas have been extended in the work of Glock and Stark (1965) into an argument that religion provides a compensation for problems and difficulties people face in their daily lives. This has been further extended by writers, including Berger, into the idea that religion provides a *sacred canopy*: that is, beliefs in the sacred which provide some overall, total explanation of human existence and which give meaning to an often confusing and chaotic world.

Evaluation activity

At the beginning of this chapter you developed a definition of religion. Would you now change it? If so, what changes would you make?
Is defining religion useful to sociologists?

The variety of definitions of religion in sociology

Some examples:

[Religion is] an attempt to explain what cannot otherwise be explained; to achieve power, when all other powers have failed; to establish poise and serenity in the face of evil and suffering that other efforts have failed to eliminate.

(Yinger 1957, p. 7)

[Religion is] a system of symbols which acts to establish powerful, persuasive modes and motivations in men by formulating conceptions of a general order of existence and clothing these conceptions with such an aura of factuality that the moods and motivations seem uniquely realistic.

(Geertz 1966, p. 4)

Religion is the human enterprise by which a sacred cosmos is established … it is the audacious attempt to conceive the entire universe as humanly significant.

(Berger 1973, pp. 33, 37)

Religion, then, consists of beliefs, actions, and institutions which assume the existence of supernatural entities with powers of action, or impersonal powers or processes possessed of moral purpose.

(Bruce 1995, p. ix)

Functional and substantive definitions again

Identify the functional and substantive elements of the definitions on page 23:

	Functional	Substantive
Geertz		
Berger		
Bruce		
Yinger		

Notice that the above definitions avoid specifying too closely what religion is and opt for rather general ideas about what it does – creating a sacred cosmos, allowing people to deal with difficult problems. None of them goes as far as Marx or Freud to claim that religion is an ideology or a neurosis. They all have a strong Weberian theme that religion is about giving meaning to social life. They all have a Durkheimian theme about the importance of the sacred.

There are some important things to notice about your own definitions and also those developed by sociologists: definitions include some things and exclude others. This is obvious, but it has important consequences.

Interpretation and application activity

Which of the following is a religion and why? You will find discussions of all these at various points in this book. You can also find information on them in most CD-ROM encyclopedias.

Islam
Scientology
Confucianism
Taoism
Socialism
Spiritualism

As we will see in Chapter 3, how we define religion influences how we measure it; we cannot measure it without knowing what we are measuring. However, a very narrow definition – religion is a belief in one God – will suggest that there is a relatively low level of **religiosity**; a wide definition – religion deals with things about which we are uncertain – will suggest high levels of religiosity.

Most of the definitions of religion have been developed by European sociologists. As we will see in Chapter 4, this has led to a concentration on Western religions and, for example, to classifications of religious organization which apply best to those religions. As we will see in Chapters 8 and 9, most of these sociologists were white men and they have had relatively little to say about the role that women and ethnic minorities play in religious organizations.

There are some lessons to be learned from the attempt to develop a useful definition:

- Good definitions are *useful* in that they help you to identify what it is you are studying.

- There *are* many religious people in the world (see Chapters 3, 6 and 7).

- There *is* a great variety of religious belief in existence (see Chapters 4, 5, 6 and 9).

● There *is* a wide variety of religious organizations in which people practise their religion (see Chapter 4).

We can end this chapter with a quotation from William James, who was a psychologist interested in religious experience:

> The very fact that there are so many [definitions of religion] and [they are] so different from one another is enough to prove that the word 'religion' cannot stand for any single principle or essence, but is rather a collective name.
>
> (James 1971, p. 39)

The lesson for sociologists here is that, although there has been a lot of effort to provide a precise definition, what we really need to do is look at the variety of ways that religion is practised, organized and believed, rather than simply try to develop inclusive definitions.

Coursework suggestion

The subject of this chapter provides a good opportunity to design small-scale questionnaires to assess how people (friends, relatives and so on) themselves define religion and what features they regard as essential to religion. You could therefore design a questionnaire which asks questions about what religion does and what its features are. You might also want to ask respondents if they are themselves religious and examine whether that affects their replies to other questions. The outcomes of a questionnaire will also provide useful material for discussions in Chapter 3 about how religion is measured.

Essay question

'Sociologists have defined religion in two ways: in terms of what religion does, and in terms of what religion is.' What are the main advantages and disadvantages of functional and substantive definitions of religion?

References and further reading

Berger, P. (1973) *The Social Reality of Religion*, Harmondsworth: Penguin.

Bruce, S. (1995) *Religion in Modern Britain*, Oxford: Oxford University Press.

Bruce, S. (1996) *Religion in the Modern World: From cathedrals to cults*, Oxford: Oxford University Press.

Coles, R. (1975) 'Football as "surrogate" religion', in M. Hills (ed.), *A Sociological Yearbook of Religion*, London: SCM Press, pp. 61–77.

Davie, G. (1997) 'The individualisation of British belief', in *Keeping the Faith, Demos*, no. 11, pp. 11–14.

Durkheim, E. (1912/1961) *The Elementary Forms of the Religious Life*, London: Allen and Unwin.

Evans-Pritchard, E.E. (1965) *Theories of Primitive Religion*, Oxford: Clarendon Press.

Freud, S. (1927/1985) 'The Future of an Illusion', in *Civilisation, Society and Religion*, The Pelican Freud Library, vol. 12, Harmondsworth: Penguin.

Geertz, C. (1966) 'Religion as a cultural system', in M. Banton (ed.), *Anthropological Approaches to the Study of Religion*, ASA Monograph 3, London: Tavistock Publications, pp. 1–44.

Glock, Y. and Stark, R. (1965) *Religion and Society in Tension*, New York: Rand McNally.

Gluckman, M. (1956) *Custom and Conflict in Africa*, Oxford: Blackwell.

Hamilton, M.B. (1995) *The Sociology of Religion*, London: Routledge.

James, W. (1971) *The Varieties of Religious Experience*, London: HarperCollins Publishers.

Lane, C. (1981) *Rites of Rulers: Ritual in industrial society, the Soviet case*, Cambridge: Cambridge University Press.

Malinowski, B. (1922) *Argonauts of the Western Pacific*, London: Routledge and Kegan Paul.

Martin, D. (1967) *The Sociology of English Religion*, London: Routledge.

Marx, K. and Engels, F. (1845/1955) *On Religion*, Moscow: Progress Publishers.

Merton, R.K. (1957) *Social Theory and Social Structure*, Glencoe: Free Press.

Parsons, T. (1951) *The Social System*, New York: Basic Books.

Radcliffe-Brown, E. (1952) 'Religion and society', in *Structure and Function in Primitive Society*, London: Cohen and West, pp. 153–77.

Simmel, G. (1898/1997) *Essays of Religion*, ed. H. Helle and L. Nierder, London: Yale University Press.

Weber, M. (1922/1968) *Economy and Society*, Berkeley: University of California Press.

Wilson, B. (1961) *Sects and Society*, London: Heinemann.

Yinger, J.M. (1957) *Religion, Society and the Individual: An introduction to the sociology of religion*, New York: Macmillan.

3 Measuring religion

Key terms	Key thinkers
Religiosity	Steve Bruce
Church membership	Grace Davie
Church attendance	
Religious belief	
Religious practice	
Believing and belonging	
Quantitative data	
Qualitative data	

Introduction

In Chapter 2, we looked at how sociologists have defined religion; in this chapter, we will look at how they have attempted to assess the extent to which people are religious. We will look at studies of religious practice and religious belief and consider some of the large amount of statistical data that is available. This chapter then provides a basis for the discussions in Chapters 6 and 7 about the alleged decline of religion.

Sociology and measuring religion

Indicators of religiosity

Sociologists of religion are interested in knowing to what extent people are religious: that is, they are interested in **religiosity**. It may seem a simple matter to decide this: collect statistics on what people do and what they believe and, perhaps, interview people about their religious beliefs and practices. However, before we can do all this we have to decide what are the main indicators of religiosity.

Sociologists have identified a number of indicators. They include membership of a religious organization; attendance at religious services; religious beliefs; how people use their religious beliefs in their daily lives; whether and how they use the religious organizations of which they are members; people's general moral and ethical views.

➤

Each of these may suggest how religious people are, but one indicator of religiosity may not completely agree with another. As we will see later, Grace Davie (1994) argues, for example, that people may **believe** but not **belong** to a church. Also, there are complex relationships between religion and morality. People do not have to be religious in order to behave morally; for example, most people, even those who say they are not religious, oppose murder.

One of the central aims of sociology is to provide statistical data. Statistical data allow sociologists to quantify things – poverty, divorce, support for political parties, the distribution of income, and so on. Collecting statistical data forms a large part of the professional life of many sociologists; such data often provide the basis on which sociologists make claims to influence social policy makers.

Application activity

Conduct a religious census of the area in which you live. How many churches and other places of worship are there? Does their number indicate the religiosity of your area? If not, what else would you need to know to assess this?

If we looked at a typical British village or city, we could conclude that religion is a very significant phenomenon in people's lives. Virtually every village has its church; in some cases, the church is built near the village school. Many schools are named after religious saints. In every city, there are many churches; some of these are cathedrals. Typically, in many cities there are places of worship of diverse faiths – Jewish synagogues, Muslim mosques, Hindu temples. On the surface, therefore, Britain seems to be a society in which religion is important. Part of the task of the

The church school remains an important feature of the British education system. But is it an indication of religiosity?

sociologist of religion is to assess levels of religiosity by measuring such things as attendance at places of worship, membership of religious organizations and religious belief. We will see how difficult this can be and how the available evidence is open to a wide range of interpretations.

We saw in Chapter 2 how our definition of religion will influence any measurement of religiosity, so we must be clear about what it is we are measuring. Usually, following Durkheim, sociologists measure belief *and* practice: that is, what people say they believe and how those beliefs are practised in particular religious organizations.

Measuring religious practice

Application activity

Ask your parents and/or grandparents if they:

- *attend a place of worship;*
- *are members of a religious organization.*

Ask them which of these they consider most important. What do the answers tell us about how we can measure religious practice?

Measuring religious practice includes the measurement of at least two things:

- Whether people are members of religious organizations. Here, we must decide what *counts* as being a member of a religious organization.

- Whether people practise their religion.

These two things may be related: people may practise their religion and also see themselves as members of a religious organization; however, people may practise their religion and still not count themselves as members of a religious organization.

We can indicate some of the issues here in the following example. Large Christian churches – the Church of England, for instance – often count their membership as including anyone who was baptised into the church. Whether those same people practise their religion when they are older is not necessarily relevant to membership. Such churches therefore have an **inclusive** idea of membership. This will indicate a relatively large membership but will tell us little, for example, about whether people go to church. Smaller religious organizations – called **sects** – usually require people to join in some active way and express their commitment; it is, therefore, more difficult to count as a member of a sect than as a member of a church. Sect membership tends to be more **exclusive** than church membership. In sects, someone might *practise* their religion for a long time and still not feel committed enough to *join* formally. (Sects are described in more detail in Chapter 4.)

Research activity

The example above is from a Christian religion. Do other religions count membership in the same way?

Measuring religious practice indicates a number of things that are very important for sociologists:

● Many people do attend places of worship.

● Attendance and membership of some religious organizations have declined over time, while others have seen increases in membership and attendance.

Table 3.1 Church summary

Church members	1975	1980	1985	1990	1994
Anglican	2,297,871	2,179,458	2,016,943	1,871,977	1,760,070
Baptist[1]	235,884	239,780	243,051	230,858	229,276
Roman Catholic	2,605,255	2,454,253,	2,279,065	2,198,694	2,002,758
Independent[1]	240,200	227,782	225,634	221,444	210,200
Methodist[1]	576,791	520,557	474,290	443,323	420,836
New Churches[1]	12,060	25,250	80,494	125,869	164,317
Orthodox	196,850	203,165	223,721	265,968	283,897
Other churches[1]	137,083	131,510	126,127	121,681	119,453
Pentecostal[1]	101,648	126,343	136,582	158,505	183,109
Presbyterian	1,589,085	1,437,775	1,322,029	1,213,920	1,120,383
Total	7,992,727	7,545,873	7,127,936	6,852,239	6,494,299
of which Free Churches	1,303,666	1,270,862	1,286,178	1,301,680	1,327,191
Percentage total is of adult population	18.5	16.9	15.5	14.7	13.9

[1] The six components of the free churches

Source: Brierley and Wraight *The UK Christian Handbook* (1995), in Davie (1997)

Figure 3.1 Adult church attendance, Britain 1851–1989

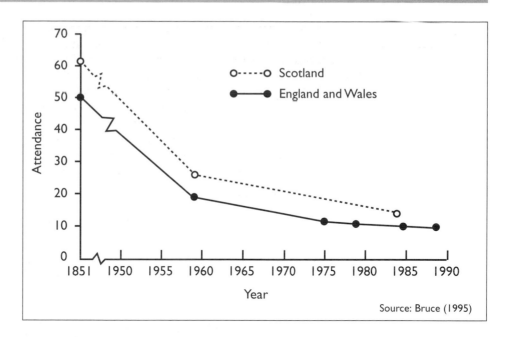

Source: Bruce (1995)

● These statistics are about membership of Christian churches in the United Kingdom between 1975 and 1994. In simple numerical terms, the pattern is clear. Some churches have seen a fall in membership: Anglican, Roman Catholic, Methodist, Presbyterian. Others, such as the Baptists, have remained fairly static. Still others (not indicated in these statistics) have experienced large increases in membership: the new Christian churches, Islam, Sikhism. We will see in Chapter 6 that sociologists disagree about how we account for these decreases and increases. However, in the case of increase in support for Islam, for example, there is some agreement that this is related to the increase in the size of the population that is of Asian origin. We will look at this in more detail in Chapter 8.

● The social organization of religious behaviour has changed over time. In Chapter 5 we will look at the development of new religious movements (NRMs) and new age movements (NAMs). We will also return to this issue when we discuss, for example, Davie's (1994) view that religion in Britain is characterized by believing without belonging; that is, many people have religious beliefs but do not belong to an identifiable religious organization.

Application and evaluation activity

Design a questionnaire to assess how much religious practice there is in your class or group. What problems arise in:

● *deciding what questions to ask?*
● *interpreting the answers?*

It is tempting to argue that religious practice indicates the extent to which people are religious; it seems obvious that if you go to a place of worship, then you are religious. However, we only have to look briefly at this idea to see that it is not as straightforward as it seems.

● How *much* religious practice counts as evidence of religiosity? Is it enough to attend a place of worship once a year, or does attendance have to be more regular? There are no definitive answers to such questions.

Membership and commitment

We will see in Chapter 6 that religious organizations themselves are increasingly concerned about membership and commitment. For example, there is concern about falling attendances and whether people who ask to be married in a religious ceremony are really religious.

Methodist church faces 'meltdown'

In today's Methodist Recorder, the membership secretary, the Rev Peter Barber, says the church is at a 'critical point in its life' and called for urgent action to avoid 'meltdown'. Training colleges could be closed because the shrinking membership is having a catastrophic impact on finances.

Over the last 15 years, the Methodists have closed more churches than any other denomination – 1,453 – and opened only 140. Since 1950 the number of Methodists has almost halved from 744,326 to 424,540. An increasingly elderly profile means more than half of the annual decline is due to death.

'This is a delayed response to previous decades and reflects the number of elderly members dying and we have not gained new members at a rate to replace them,' said the Rev Brian Beck, secretary of the Methodist Conference. 'There is no point running away from it, we must face the decline and its very important consequences. If it goes on at this rate, we will not be able to maintain the structure of the church.'

METHODIST DECLINE
Membership figures of the Methodist Church in thousands.

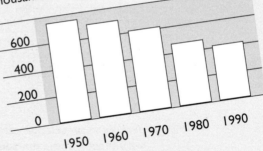

THE YOUNG METHODISTS
Aged 26 and under involved with the Methodist Church in thousands.

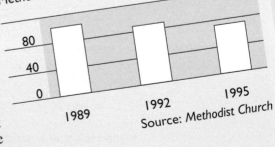

Source: Methodist Church

Source: Adapted from *The Guardian*, 18 October 1997

- Which practices count as signs of *religious* practice? For example, does a person who regularly attends church at Christmas count as religious? Does getting married in church count, even though you are not a regular churchgoer? Does a Muslim woman who agrees, for her parents' sake, to a religious marriage ceremony, count as religious? These are particularly interesting questions for sociologists, because some Church of England clergy, for example, ask people who do want to marry in church to attend regularly before they are married, almost as a test of religious commitment.

Practising your religion at home

As we will see in Chapter 4, there is much more to religion than simply attending at a place of worship. In effect, the place where people practise may not be particularly significant. The development of the Christian House Church Movement in the UK, where groups of people celebrate their religion in their homes, indicates this. They are not *necessarily* less religious because they celebrate their religion at home.

There is a broader issue here, which was first discussed by Max Weber (1904/1974). In his analysis of Protestantism and Calvinism, Weber was concerned not only with the role that religious ethics played in the development of capitalism (see Chapter 10), but also with the attitudes of Protestants and Calvinists to religion itself. What he noticed was that both of these religious groups had a distinct idea of what counted as religious. This included the idea that every legitimate activity was religious if it was what God wanted people to do. It also included the idea that going to church and worshipping as a way of influencing God was theologically misguided. In other words, you could be religious by working hard in your job and, as it were, dedicating your life to God. Religious worship in church thus becomes less important as a measure of religiosity.

There is a further point for Weber. Calvinism argued that people were predestined by God at birth either to be saved or damned. Nothing a person did could alter this decision, nor could a person discover what the decision was. This, of course, implied that a great deal of religious worship and the role of religious practitioners – priests, vicars and so on – were no longer relevant. We might find the idea of a religion where worship and clergy are unimportant rather strange. As sociologists, the views of Luther and Calvin point to some of the difficulties we have in measuring religion.

- Is there more to attending worship than its religious roles? Historians of religion in the UK have noted that, in the sixteenth and seventeenth centuries, very large numbers of people attended church regularly, but have asked whether that attendance had other functions. For example, the church was the major community organization and attendance was expected, whatever the level of a person's commitment. The issue here is the one to which Durkheim and Marx drew attention: if being religious is, for the sociologist, much more than a certain form of practice or belief, that would apply both now and in the past. In other words, there were *always* wider social functions for church membership. As we will see later, the difference is that now there is a much greater variety of religious and non-religious beliefs to entice people.

● Many people now seem to attend religious worship solely at significant points in their lives – births, marriages, deaths – that is, for **rites of passage**. Many more people do this than attend worship regularly. These rites of passage were much more important in premodern societies. However, in the modern world, there is still some recognition of the importance of some changes of status and many of these occur in a religious environment.

Many rites of passage still require a religious setting.

Research and interpretation activity

Ask your parents and friends if they attend religious worship. If they do, ask them why and try to identify the religious reasons and the non-religious ones.

It is important to be aware of these difficulties in measuring religious practice and, consequently, to be aware of the difficulties that we face in interpreting statistics about religious practice.

Interpretation activity

Do the statistics on pp. 30–1 indicate that people are less religious than they used to be? Give three reasons for your interpretation.

We can summarize this complex picture by distinguishing between four groups of people: those who are non-religious; those who are nominal Christians; those who are active church members; and those who are members of other religious communities. Grace Davie (1994) provides the following summary table:

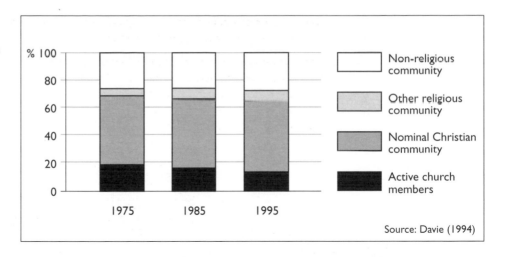

Figure 3.2 Religious components of the population (adapted from Brierley and Hiscock 1993)

Source: Davie (1994)

Application activity

*Using this book and other sources, identify the other religious communities to which Davie refers. What do you think Davie means by **nominal** and **active**? Does this distinction apply to the other religious communities you have identified? What does the table tell us about:*

- *the extent of religious practice in Britain between 1975 and 1995?*
- *how religious people are in Britain?*

Measuring religious belief

The other aspect of religion that sociologists have studied is religious **belief**. Sociologists may ask questions such as 'Do you believe in God?' or 'Do you believe in an after-life?' The first thing to note is that such questions are likely to be more difficult to answer and interpret than questions such as 'Do you own your own home?' or 'Do you believe in home ownership?' Second, it is noticeable again that these questions are closely tied to the sociologists' definition of religion. The statistics provided in Tables 3.2 and 3.3 indicate the wide range of questions which sociologists can ask about religious belief.

Table 3.2 Indicators of religious commitment, Great Britain compared with European average, percentages

Indicators of religious disposition	Great Britain		European average		Indicators of orthodox beliefs	Great Britain		European average	
	1981	1990	1981	1990		1981	1990	1981	1990
Often think about meaning and purposes of life	34	36	30	33	Believe in personal God	31	32	32	39
Often think about death	15	19	18	20	Believe in a spirit or lifeforce	39	41	36	30
Need moments of prayer, etc.	50	53	57	60	Believe in:				
Define self as a religious person	58	54	62	63	God	76	71	73	72
Draw comfort or strength from religion	46	44	48	48	Sin	69	68	57	54
					Soul	59	64	57	61
God is important in my life	50	44	51	52	Heaven	57	53	40	42
					Life after death	45	44	43	44
					The devil	30	30	25	26
					Hell	27	25	23	23

Source: Timms, *Family and Citizenship: Values in Contemporary Britain* (1992), in Davie (1997)

Table 3.3 Superstitions, Britain 1991 (%)			
Propositions	**'Definitely' and 'Probably true'**	**'Probably' and 'Definitely false'**	**'I can't choose' and 'No answer'**
Good luck charms sometimes do bring good luck	22	72	6
Some fortune tellers really can foresee the future	40	53	8
Some faith healers really do have God-given, healing powers	45	45	10
A person's star sign at birth, or horoscope, can affect the course of their future	28	64	9

Source: British Social Attitudes Survey (1991)

We can see from these figures that many people believe things that look, in one way or another, to be religious or something close to religious.

Interpretation activity

Look at the information provided in Tables 3.2 and 3.3. Rank these beliefs on a five-point scale.

Religious	**Superstitious**

Compare your rankings with those of other people in your group. How much agreement is there on these rankings? To what extent do the various rankings affect our view, as sociologists, of the extent of religious belief?

There are some important trends in belief that we need to look at more closely.

● The extent of religious belief varies between societies; more people in the United States say they believe in God than do people in the UK. We will look at this further in Chapters 6, 7 and 8. Statistics from the European Value Studies carried out in 1981 and 1990 (Table 3.2 above) indicate differences between the UK and Europe. European averages indicate that people in Europe are more likely than those in the UK to see God as important in their lives and to need moments of prayer; they are also more likely to believe in a personal God. Some countries in Europe – France and the Netherlands, for example – have much higher proportions of people who say they have no religious affiliation than do others – Italy and Spain, for example (Davie 1994, pp. 10–12).

Interpretation activity

Examine Table 3.2 and indicate three other significant differences between religious belief in the UK and Europe. How useful are averages of this kind in assessing the significance of religious belief?

- Different religions seem to have greater or lesser amounts of religious belief. Roman Catholics, for example, are more likely than members of the Church of England to say they believe in God.

- Religious belief seems to have declined over time: for example, belief in a life after death declined significantly in Britain between 1951 and 1991.

- Other beliefs – in fortune telling or faith healing – are important.

What we should notice here is that:

- More people claim to have religious beliefs than say they practise their religion, in the sense of going to a place of worship.

- Many people have beliefs in something other-worldly (remember Weber's very simple definition of religion discussed in Chapter 2, p. 18–19), but which are less obviously religious. For example, it is estimated that 35 per cent of the population of the United States believe in flying saucers and a proportion of those claim to have been abducted by aliens (Showalter 1997). It is unclear whether, from the point of view of established religions, all such other-worldly beliefs count as religious. Does a belief in witches, ghosts or the healing power of crystals count as a religious belief? Do such beliefs fulfil religious functions? Whereas many religions are likely to regard a belief in ghosts, for example, as evidence for an increase in paganism, people who have such beliefs may regard them as religious.

- Religious beliefs have, themselves, become less specific and more abstract. An example here is the contrast between the ten commandments in the Old Testament of the Christian Bible and the commandments given in the New Testament. The ten commandments are very specific and make sense in the context of a close-knit, rural community – not stealing animals, for example, makes sense for rural communities. In the New Testament there are fewer commandments and they are more abstract. For example, the commandment to love your neighbour can be meaningful to *any* believer, whatever his or her occupation or interests. Although there may be a theological reason for the change, what interests sociologists is the social reason; that is, the need for a religion to appeal to a wider audience with very varied occupations. This has a cost. The more abstract religious beliefs become, the more difficult it is to distinguish them from other, non-religious beliefs. A religious ethic which says that you should be kind to neighbours and strangers alike looks very much like the non-religious ethic of humanism, for example.

Research activity

Using a variety of sources (including CD-ROMs, encyclopedias and other books), identify the central beliefs of humanism. How far are these distinct from religious beliefs?

As we will see in Chapter 6, problems connected with the measurement of religious practice and belief are also connected with the debate about secularization, which is about whether religion has declined and/or changed its social functions. As Steve Bruce (1996, p. 27) argues, measuring how religious we are is a very modern thing to do. Not only is the collection of statistical data of very recent origin, but also measurement of religion has only occurred when a series of belief systems compete with religion. In medieval Europe, for example, membership of churches was taken for granted and no one tried to measure it. In that sense, *everyone* was religious. We will come back to the issue of just how religious people were in the past in Chapter 6.

Who practises and who believes?

Having *measured* religious belief and practice, it is also important to look at *who* practises and believes. Bruce (1995, pp. 42–4, 52–4), in an analysis of material from the British Social Attitudes surveys, suggests that not everyone practises and believes in equal measure. In addition, there are differences in who *practises* religion and who has religious *beliefs*.

Who practises?

Not all social groups practise religion to the same degree. Women are more likely to do so than men: 60 per cent of Christian churchgoers in Britain are women and nearly 66 per cent of *regular* churchgoers are women. People aged 15–44 are much more likely to attend Christian worship than those who are younger or older. Highly educated, middle-class people are also more likely to attend church. Finally, ethnic minorities are more likely to practise religion. We will return to the issues of gender and ethnicity in Chapters 8 and 9.

Table 3.4 Gender and church attendance, Britain and Northern Ireland, 1991 (%)

Attendance	Britain			Northern Ireland	
	Men	Women		Men	Women
Frequent	37	63		39	61
Regular	35	65		57	43
Rare	48	52		49	51

Source: British Social Attitudes Survey (1991), in Bruce (1995)

A typical congregation?

Figure 3.3 Church attendance, by age, England (1991) and Scotland (1984)

Sources: Brierley, *'Christian' England: What the English Church Census Reveals* (1991); Church of Scotland Board of Social Responsibility, *Lifestyle Survey* (1987), in Bruce (1995)

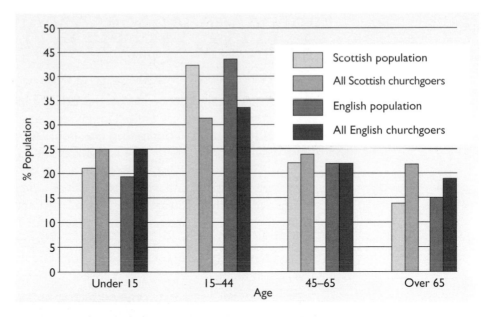

Table 3.5 Social class and church attendance, Britain, 1991 (%)		
Attendance	**Non-manual**	**Manual**
Fortnightly or more	16	12
Monthly – once a year	29	24
Less than once a year	3	4
Never	48	57
No answer	3	3

Source: British Social Attitudes Survey (1991), in Bruce (1995)

Who believes?

Patterns of believing do not always correlate with patterns of practising religion. For example, men and women *believe* in almost equal measure. Wealthier and more middle-class people are less likely to believe in God than those who are poorer, even though they are *more* likely to practise a religion. In other words, as far as occupation and social class are concerned, patterns of belief and patterns of practice run in opposite directions. In addition, the nature of belief seems to have become more abstract, fewer people believing in a personal God and more believing in some vague, supernatural lifeforce.

Bruce sums up the relationship between who practises and who believes in the following way:

> The middle classes are much more decisive in their religious behaviour and narrow in their use of terms to describe it. More middle-class than working-class people are involved with the churches, but those who are not are less likely than their working-class counterparts to claim religious beliefs or describe themselves as religious.

> (Bruce 1995, pp. 52–3)

Methodological problems

A lot of statistical evidence has been presented in this chapter. Two methodological issues are important about these data. First, great care has to be taken in **designing** questions. An obvious example here would be the need to take account of the variety of religions in Britain. The question 'Do you attend worship on a Sunday?' would be meaningless to someone who was Jewish or a Seventh Day Adventist, neither of whom see Sunday as a particularly important day in religious terms. It would also be meaningless for Muslims, who are most likely to attend mosque on a Friday, or to Hindus, who may attend temple (Mandir) on many occasions but also practise their religion at home.

Second, there may be problems in **interpreting** the answers to questionnaires. These include the problem of deciding whether the answers *do* indicate religiosity, but also the problem of knowing whether people are giving accurate, reliable answers. If, for example, attending worship is an accepted form of behaviour in a community, people may be inclined to say they attend even if, in reality, they often do not do so.

Conclusion

This chapter had two aims: to look at some of the statistical data on religious belief and practice, and to suggest that such data are neither easy to gather nor easy to interpret. As a sociologist, you need to be aware of the difficulties of both data collection and data analysis. You should be able to look at a table of statistics and say:

- this is what these statistics mean;
- this is what they do not tell us.

You should develop a healthy scepticism with regard to data. In the sociology of religion such scepticism is particularly important given that much of the available data is from Christian religions, reflecting the fact that Christianity is the dominant state religion.

The statistical picture of religious practice and belief is complex, but it should not lead us to reject the data entirely. They tell us *something* about religious practice and belief, if not everything we want to know. We will see in Chapters 6 and 7, for example, that the available statistics have led some sociologists to say that religion has become less important and some to deny this claim. The statistics themselves cannot provide the definitive answer.

Coursework suggestion

Opportunities for coursework include looking at the degree of religious diversity in your locality, in order both to get away from the focus on Christianity, which is a part of the sociology of religion, and to find out whether different religions have different ways of assessing religiosity. You could also try to collect your own statistics on religion, using the two main methods employed by sociologists: collecting quantitative statistical data (by means of questionnaires, for example) and collecting qualitative data (by means of interviews, for example). You may want to decide which, if any, of these methods provides the most useful data.

Essay question

Is it possible to measure religious belief and practice without defining religion? How do different definitions influence how we measure religion?

DATA RESPONSE QUESTIONS

There is no one reliable way of measuring churchgoing. It is prohibitively expensive to place enumerators outside a sufficiently large number of churches to be sure that their counting is representative. So we either survey a sample of the general public and ask them how often they go to church or we ask clergymen to estimate the size of their congregations. The general survey has the weakness that respondents may exaggerate their churchgoing as they give what they feel are the expected answers. Contrary to what we might expect, priests, ministers and pastors do not exaggerate their popularity. When researchers have set out to elicit claims of attendance in surveys and test them against clergy estimates, they have found the survey data overestimating by between 50 and 100 per cent.

(Bruce 1995, pp. 38–9)

Look again at the statistics presented on pp. 30–1 and 35–6 and answer the following questions.

1 Why does Bruce claim that surveys overestimate such things as attendance at church worship?

2 *Bruce's argument applies almost exclusively to Christian religions. Are there any reasons why his argument might not apply to other religions?*

3 *What do the statistics tell us about religious practice and religious belief in Britain?*

4 *Does what Bruce says invalidate the statistics? If not, why not?*

References and further reading

Barker, E., Halman, L. and Vloet, A. (1993) *The European Values Study, 1981–1990, Summary Report*, London/Netherlands: EVS Group.

Bruce, S. (1995) *Religion in Modern Britain*, Oxford: Oxford University Press.

Bruce, S. (1996) *Religion in the Modern World: From cathedrals to cults*, Oxford: Oxford University Press.

Davie, G. (1994) *Religion in Britain since 1945: Believing without belonging*, Oxford: Blackwell.

Davie, G. (1997) 'The individualisation of British belief', in *Keeping the Faith*, *Demos*, no. 11, pp. 11–14.

Hamilton, M.B. (1995) *The Sociology of Religion*, London: Routledge.

Showalter, E. (1997) *Hystories: Hysteria, Gender and Culture*, London: Picador.

Weber, M. (1904/1974) *The Protestant Ethic and the Spirit of Capitalism*, London: Unwin.

4 Religious organizations

<table>
<tr><td>

Key terms
Church
Denomination
Sect
Cult
Ecclesia
Charisma

</td><td>

Key thinkers
Ernst Troeltsch
Max Weber
Reinhold Niebuhr
Bryan Wilson
Georg Simmel
Charles Glock and Rodney Stark
Roy Wallis
Ernest Becker
Rodney Stark and William Bainbridge

</td></tr>
</table>

Introduction

This chapter looks at what sociologists have said about how religion is organized. It identifies the main forms of religious institution – the church, the denomination, the sect and the cult – and indicates how these institutions relate to each other. The limitations of these classifications are also looked at, particularly the fact that they were developed in the context of Western, Christian religions and may not be appropriate to the other world religions – Hinduism and Buddhism, for example.

Churches, denominations, sects and cults

As with other aspects of social life, religion is socially organized; it has its own institutions, for example the church. Sociologists have identified four major forms of religious organization: the church, the denomination, the sect and the cult. The first thing to notice is that some of these terms are used outside sociology; some, particularly Christian, religious organizations use the term 'church' to describe themselves. This can become confusing, as in the following examples: there is the Roman Catholic Church, which is usually defined by sociologists as a church; there is the Unification Church, which, for sociologists, is a sect; and there is the Methodist Church, which most sociologists would call a denomination. None of these is a cult, but the term 'cult' also has its sociological and non-sociological uses. As we will see in Chapter 5, since the 1970s new forms of religious organization have developed: these have usually been called new religious movements (NRMs) and new age movements (NAMs).

The above classification of religious organizations developed out of the work of Weber, Troeltsch (1931/1976) and Niebuhr (1962). Although, as we saw in Chapter 2,

Weber was interested in a range of world religions, Troeltsch and Niebuhr were mainly interested in the religions of the Western world. This means that we have to be wary about whether the classification of religious organizations applies to many world religions – for example, Buddhism, Hinduism or Confucianism.

Eurocentrism

There is an issue here about how focused sociology was and is on understanding those societies which were the first to become modern, complex, industrial societies – that is, Britain, other countries in Europe, and the United States. Sociology is often described as Eurocentric. In the sociology of religion, for example, Troeltsch and Niebuhr were almost exclusively interested in Christian religions and their development in Europe and the United States. This raises a very important question: how far is what Troeltsch and Niebuhr argued applicable to other religions that are not Christian and to the many religions (for example, Hinduism) that do not believe solely in one God?

We will now look at how sociologists have understood these four organizational types. Note that they are models of religious organizations which indicate *typical* features; not all examples will have all these features. They are what Weber called 'ideal types'. An ideal type of a religious organization – for example, a church – would identify the typical features of a range of churches. Not all churches would fit the type exactly. Ideal types are useful because they show what all churches have in common and they also highlight their differences. The Church of England and the Roman Catholic Church are both churches in terms of the ideal type, but they also have distinguishing features, such as different religious practitioners and different forms of worship. The discussion of various religious organizations in this chapter is based upon ideal types that sociologists have found *useful* to aid analysis and discussion.

Ideal types

Weber developed the ideal-type method because he realized that studying society was very complex and difficult. Sociology is unlike the 'natural sciences' – physics, for example – in that it is difficult to conduct experiments on people and social groups. Indeed, the very act of studying social groups can change how they behave. The ideal type is a model that contains the features of a range of real types. For example, the ideal type of a church (see below) has a number of features to which any real church will only approximate. In common with many other social scientists – for example, economists who study the workings of markets and patterns of demand and supply – sociologists find that the ideal type is an invaluable tool for studying

➤

how the real world works. According to Weber, sociologists who wish to study social life have only two alternatives:

> The only choice is often between a terminology which is not clear at all and one which is clear but unrealistic, an 'ideal type'. In this situation, the latter sort of terminology is scientifically preferable.
>
> (Runciman 1978, p. 25)

The church

Examples:
Church of England, Roman Catholic Church, Islam

Weber and Troeltsch identified a number of features which make churches distinct from other forms of religious organization:

● Large membership;

● inclusive;

● bureaucratic;

● professional clergy;

● acceptance of wider society;

● a monopoly of the truth.

Churches tend to be *big*. For example, in the fifteenth century in Europe, Catholicism was *the* religion, with a huge membership and great political power. The Church of England estimated its membership in 1994 to be about 1.7 million. There are thought to be 1.2 million Muslims in Britain and half a million Hindus. Each of these figures is more than the combined membership of the three main political parties in the United Kingdom. While there are difficulties in deciding what 'membership' means, membership of churches is nevertheless still significant in statistical terms (see Chapter 3).

Churches tend also to be *inclusive* and have what we can call *involuntary membership*. If, for example, children are born of parents who belong to the Church of England, and are baptised, they will usually be counted as members. This may be confirmed by their attending church with their parents. They do not actively choose to be members. The church includes large numbers of such involuntary members. In effect, such members do not have to show how religious they are in any rigorous sense – no one is likely to test whether they agree with what the church believes, something that often *does* happen in religious sects.

Because they tend to be big and may cover several different societies, churches tend also to be *bureaucratic*. In other words, they are hierarchies with most power at the top. Like most bureaucracies, they have professionals in them; in the case of churches, these include priests, bishops, vicars, rabbis, imams and so on, who must undergo training to prepare them for their professional duties.

Generally, churches *accept the wider society* and are more likely than sects, for example, to support the state and the status quo. They allow members to have reasonably free dealings with the wider society, although they may ask members to behave in a religious manner when dealing with other people. Put another way, church membership requires only a partial commitment on the part of the believer: unless you become a priest, for example, you will not be required to devote your whole life to religious pursuits and rules, which include celibacy in some churches.

Finally, churches claim to have a monopoly of the truth: they claim to have the correct view of things as opposed to other religious and non-religious belief systems.

The sect

Examples:
Christian Science, the Salvation Army, Quakers, the Amish

- Small, exclusive membership;

- total commitment;

- some opposition to wider society;

- nno professional clergy;

- charismatic leader/founder.

Sects are, in many ways, the opposite of churches in everything except their belief that they have a monopoly on the truth. As with churches, sects will deny that what other sects and non-religious organizations say is true; only the sect can guarantee that people who join will, for example, be saved from the evils of the wider society.

Sects are usually relatively small and their small size can be explained in terms of their claim to have some unique view of the truth. Another of the founders of sociology, Georg Simmel, saw smallness as an essential feature of the sect; it has to be small because it depends upon close links between members and an oppositional stance towards the wider society (Wolff 1964). Also, membership is exclusive: only people who know the truth and actively commit themselves to it count as members. This gives the sect its rationale – we know the truth and the majority of non-members do not – and its way of dealing with the wider society. Sects are much more likely than churches to reject what the wider society has to say and to be hostile to that wider society. The Amish, who formed small communities in the United States, reject almost all of modern technology – cars, zips and radios, for example. Members are asked to give their total commitment to the sect and this may include giving up their income for the benefit of the sect. Being small, sects are rarely bureaucratic and rarely have a professional clergy separate from the ordinary members.

The Amish people of Pennsylvania reject modern technology. Their clothing and customs have changed little since 1700.

When sects develop they may well do so because of the central role of a charismatic figure, who claims that the established church is in some way in error. Weber (in Gerth and Mills 1948) argues that all sects are originally based on personal charisma: that is, on a leader who has special qualities, which followers see as inspirational (see pp. 50–2 and 154–5 for a full discussion of charisma).

The denomination

Examples:
Methodism, the Baptist movement

- Large, inclusive membership;

- bureaucratic;

- professional clergy;

- acceptance of wider society;

- acceptance of religious diversity;

- no monopoly of the truth.

Denominations are usually smaller than churches and bigger than sects. They recognize a typical feature of the modern world – the vast range of things that people can believe – and do not, unlike the church and sect, claim any monopoly over what people believe. Put another way, it is very difficult in the modern world, with all its belief systems, for any one of them to *claim* to be correct and *sustain* that claim.

There are two other features of denominations that are important. First, they ask for a low level of commitment from members, a commitment closer to that required by a church than that required by a sect. Second, because they are tolerant and open to other people's beliefs, they are often difficult to distinguish from one another. As we will see in Chapters 5 and 6, more and more religious organizations are resembling denominations in their tolerance of other beliefs and their unwillingness to specify too precisely exactly what they believe. This is one of the reasons for the development of forms of religious fundamentalism and the support for religious sects.

The cult

Examples:
Transcendental meditation, Spiritualism

- Small;

- individualistic;

- mystical;

- pragmatic;

- informal;

- short-lived.

There is considerably less discussion in sociology about cults. However, in popular discussions of religious movements, the cult is presented as a problem. In many cases, an organization which, for the sociologist, would be a sect – a small movement, requiring total commitment and total separation from the wider society – is popularly called a cult. An example is the Branch-Davidian movement in the United States, whose headquarters in Waco, Texas, were beseiged by police in 1993. We will explore the popular, media presentation of cults in more detail in Chapter 5 (see pp. 58–9).

Troeltsch (1931/1976) identified three types of religious organization, two of which – the church and the sect – we have already discussed. He described a third type in terms of mysticism: this is an unorganized, voluntary association that emphasizes individualism. In other words, people join for individual, often pragmatic reasons, for example, to achieve some practical end. In addition, this form of religious organization is non-radical, in that it does not challenge the wider society and its appeal is mainly to people who are socially privileged. As we will see, this form of organization is very like what sociologists now call a cult.

Perhaps the clearest sociological discussion of cults is found in the work of Stark and Bainbridge (1985), who distinguish between audience cults, client cults and cultic movements. **Audience cults** are the most individualistic and unorganized; astrology is a good example, particularly as much of it is sustained through the mass media. **Client cults** are more organized and provide a service to members; a good example is Spiritualism, which has the basic aim of allowing people to contact the dead. **Cultic movements** come closest to sects in the way that they are organized and offer a range of both spiritual and material support to members. Scientology is a possible example of a cultic movement, although it has many of the attributes of NRMs and sects.

Archbishop urges end to 'cult of Diana'

The Archbishop of York has called for the cult of Diana, Princess of Wales to end, warning that the country is in danger of 'clinging too much to the icon'.

David Hope, the second-most senior bishop in the Church of England, has also launched a scathing attack on the Diana museum opened last week by the princess's brother, Earl Spencer, on his Althorp estate in Northamptonshire. The archbishop said: 'It's the last thing she would have wanted.'... After seeing pictures of the Diana temple – which includes a black silhouette of her head – Hope said he was concerned at the cult growing up around her memory. 'We should be careful that she is not worshipped. That worship should be directed to the God who created her.'

'If people have a particular memory of Diana they should honour this by getting in touch with the charities she championed. Her compassion and her care are the things we should be reflecting on as a society, not just indulging our emotions.'

Source: *The Sunday Times*, 5 July 1998

Interpretation activity

In the light of the sociological definition and classification of cults given above, to what extent is there 'a cult of Diana'?

Wallis (1976) provides one of the best ways of making sense of this complex classification:

Internal conception \ External conception	Respectable	Deviant
Uniquely legitimate	**Church**	**Sect**
Pluralistically legitimate	**Denomination**	**Cult**

For Wallis, there are two particularly important issues in the analysis of religious organization. An organization's **internal conception** refers to how the organization regards its own beliefs and practices. Its **external conception** refers to how the organization is regarded by the wider society.

The church and the sect have the same internal conception: that is, they claim to have the truth. The denomination and cult, on the other hand, recognize a range of versions of the truth. Therefore, church and sect claim to be uniquely legitimate; denomination and cult claim pluralistic legitimacy. In terms of external conception, the church and denomination have in common that they are generally seen as respectable; the sect and the cult are seen as deviant.

Application activity

Using this book and other resources – including CD-ROMs and the Internet – identify two examples of each of these types of religious organization.

The many classifications of organizations

There is, in fact, a large number of classifications of religious organizations, most of which develop those identified by Troeltsch and Weber. Becker (1932), for example, identifies four types of religious organization: the ecclesia, the sect, the denomination and the cult. The **ecclesia** is close to what we have described as the church, and for Becker there are two types: the national ecclesia (for example, Anglicanism) and the international ecclesia (for example, Roman Catholicism).

Yinger (1957) develops a more complex typology: the universal church, the ecclesia, the denomination, the established sect, the sect and the cult. There are also three types of sect: acceptance sects, aggressive sects and avoidance sects.

These various typologies are not, in any simple sense, right or wrong. What you should decide is whether they are *useful* in understanding the variety of religious organizations which you, as a sociologist, might study.

The church/sect dynamic

As Wallis (1976) indicates, one of the most important issues in looking at religious organizations is how they relate to the wider, non-church world. There is, in fact, a complex set of relationships between churches, sects and the wider society which tells us a lot about how religious organizations develop and change.

We can look first at what Weber said about religious sects, about how they develop and the role of what he called **charisma**. The first thing for Weber is that, whereas churches tend to represent those with privilege and power, sects tend to represent and get the support of those who lack power and privilege – that is, the underprivileged. This, for Weber, is the origin of Christianity, which developed as a

sect in opposition to the state religion of the Roman Empire. The more the church supports the state and the status quo, the less it is able to represent those who lack power; there is therefore likely to be a need among those groups for a different form of religious organization and belief. This means that all churches are likely to experience sectarian breakaways; they are part of the normal life history of churches.

Weber takes a further step by arguing that the experience of underprivilege is not enough on its own to guarantee the development of a religious sect. What is also needed is a leader who is charismatic. Again the model here is early Christianity. Sociologists are, of course, interested in what early Christians believed, but they would also draw attention to the figure of Jesus Christ as a charismatic figure. For Weber, charisma has two aspects: people with charisma have some special feature ascribed to them by followers (for example, the power to heal people), and this feature or features is or are unique to that person. Charisma is:

> an *extraordinary* quality of a person, regardless of whether this quality is actual, alleged, or presumed.
>
> (Gerth and Mills 1948, p. 295)

Wilson elaborates on this:

> Charisma denotes a quality not of the individual, but a relationship between believers (or followers) and the man in whom they believe. ... Charisma is not a personality attribute, but a successful claim to power by virtue of supernatural ordination.
>
> (Wilson 1975, p. 7)

Charisma has four interesting features. First, it often provides the basis for the growth of a new religious sect that breaks away from an established church. The leader will be responding to the needs of followers for this breakaway. An individual might claim charisma, but if there is no potential group of followers then nothing is likely to happen. Thus, the development of a sect requires a group that sees itself as underprivileged *and* which has a potential leader; neither, on its own, guarantees sect development. Underprivilege may be related to fairly objective factors – poverty, unemployment, racial oppression, gender oppression – as well as to feelings of underprivilege.

Second, charisma is by its very nature unstable. Because it is unique to an individual – Weber refers to this as personal charisma – and it is what gives that person his or her position in a sect, then charisma cannot, in any simple way, be passed on to someone else. This suggests two related problems, both of which Weber discussed in terms of the **routinization of charisma** and the development of the **charisma of office**. If the sect wishes to gain a wider appeal it needs to take its message beyond the original group; to do this it needs some form of social organization and may need to alter its message to make it more appealing to more people. This need to recruit more widely tends to make sects more bureaucratic. Charisma is then increasingly seen as something belonging to the office holder, whoever he or she is. Its unique, personal qualities begin to weaken.

In addition, charismatic leaders, like everyone else, die. There is then a problem of who succeeds the leader, because the charisma cannot be transmitted to someone else; it is *unique* to the original leader. The process of succession itself becomes routinized; succession may become hereditary or based upon some form of election. Both of these weaken the original magic and special nature of the charisma. As we will see in Chapter 6, this process of routinization is part of the general process of secularization. We will also see in Chapter 10 how charismatic breakthrough is one way of explaining how religion relates to processes of social change (see pp. 154–5).

The death of charismatic leaders

The above is a sociological account of charisma. What goes on in many sects is a process by which the members themselves deal with the death of the leader. In many cases – for example, Christianity and Rastafarianism – members believe that the leader has not really died; he or she is believed still to exist in a spiritual sense and, crucially, still to have a role to play in the daily life of members. The leader who succeeds the original charismatic figure is then seen as that figure's representative.

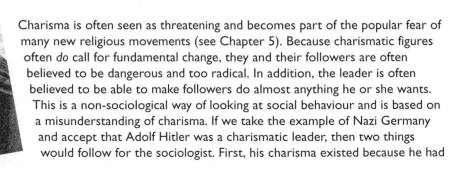

Charisma is often seen as threatening and becomes part of the popular fear of many new religious movements (see Chapter 5). Because charismatic figures often *do* call for fundamental change, they and their followers are often believed to be dangerous and too radical. In addition, the leader is often believed to be able to make followers do almost anything he or she wants. This is a non-sociological way of looking at social behaviour and is based on a misunderstanding of charisma. If we take the example of Nazi Germany and accept that Adolf Hitler was a charismatic leader, then two things would follow for the sociologist. First, his charisma existed because he had a group of followers; without those followers no claim to charisma would have been effective. Second, it is difficult to see how, as a charismatic figure, Hitler alone could have done what he did without a large group of followers.

Finally, the term 'charisma' is now used very widely indeed and in a way that is not very sociologically useful. To assert that footballers, politicians, actors and so on are charismatic is to miss several points: that charisma is about breaking away from established ways of doing things; that these examples rarely have the extraordinary, magical powers which Weber discusses; that they do not lead significant social movements.

Thinking sociologically

As with 'church', the term 'charisma' is used both in sociology *and* outside it. It is important, if you are to think sociologically, to keep these two different uses distinct.

Application activity

Make a list of charismatic figures. What do they have in common? Do all religions have charismatic figures?

We can look at Bryan Wilson's classification of religious sects as an example of how different religious sects relate to and deal with the wider society. Table 1.1 shows how Wilson (1982) identifies seven types of sect. Some of these sects will be mentioned below. You will be able to find out about them in Wilson's work. However, you should also be able to find information about them from a variety of sources, including the Internet and CD-ROM encyclopedias.

Sects are likely to have problems in dealing with the wider society, particularly as they often disagree, for example, with established religions and claim to have a new version of the truth. Sects can therefore withdraw from the wider world, as with Pietism; they can engage with the wider world by seeking to change it, as with revolutionist sects like the Christadelphians; they can engage with the wider world without seeking to change it or convert people, as in the case of reformist sects like the Quakers. These alternatives are, in part, determined by what the wider world does: for example, a violently anti-sect reaction from the wider world may lead to withdrawal.

For Wilson, the importance of the relationship between sects and the wider society lies in the fact that sects change over time, depending on how this relationship develops. Sects may start out as revolutionist and try to change the world. If they fail, they may become utopian, with some ideal view of a future world, but no clear way to achieve it; or they may become reformist, with a programme to reform society through religious activity, rather than fundamentally changing it. Quakers, for example, used to be more revolutionary than they are now. Not only do sects change their orientation to the wider society, they may also develop into churches – as with Christianity – or into denominations. They may also experience their own sectarian breakaway: for example, the Amish in the United States are now split into one group that wants to compromise with the wider society and another that wants to remain faithful to the original message. Finally, of course, sects may disappear altogether;

Table 4.1 The typology of sects

Conversionist *Example: the Salvation Army*	As their name implies, these sects actively seek to convert people. This is an obvious way of increasing membership but also brings the sect into conflict with both other religions and those who are not religious. Early Christianity was conversionist and, like many conversionist sects, rapidly became a church with a more formal structure and a claim to inclusive, rather than	exclusive, membership. Contemporary conversionist sects emphasize religious revival in a world in which religion has become less important: this revival is centred on preaching the original, fundamental message. There is believed to be a strong personal relationship between the believer and the saviour, and conversion is rapid.
Revolutionist *Examples: Christadelphians, Jehovah's Witnesses*	These usually emphasize conversion but take a more radical stance towards the wider society. They are more likely to portray that society as evil and dangerous and wish for the overthrow of the existing order of things. When the world is overturned, the sect members will become powerful. Therefore membership of the sect guarantees salvation. These sects are hostile to social reform through religion and believe in a slow, rather than a rapid, conversion to sect	beliefs. This slow conversion also involves strict tests of membership and a stress on the purity and sacredness of sect beliefs. Predictions about the future and about imminent salvation are related to contemporary events which are seen as signs that change is just around the corner. The view of God in these sects is of an autocratic dictator who controls the universe and is not open to control by the sect.
Introversionist *Example: Pietism*	These are sects that withdraw from the world and are indifferent to social reform and to conversion. Rather than trying to change things, members aim for a deeper spiritual experience	and for inner change: there is a strong element of self-mastery and self-discipline. Ideas of God do not include the idea of a personal God who can be influenced but some sort of holy spirit.
Manipulationist *Examples: Christian Science, Scientology*	These sects believe that members can have access to some special knowledge or technique which can achieve social ends. Individuals can use this knowledge or technique and they do not need a special relationship with the movement, a God or saviour. Where the members do come together, they do so as a way to claim status and prestige and to show how successful the sect is in improving people's status in the wider society. Anyone can learn the	knowledge and techniques if they are willing to undergo what is often a long and expensive training. There is no belief in a personal God or saviour and the sect's beliefs are often a mix of religious and non-religious traditions. Where they make claims to deal with illness, they come into conflict with medicine, for example over opposition to the use of blood transfusions. These are the least religious looking of the sects and have been called *cults*.
Thaumaturgical *Example: Spiritualism*	Their belief is that the supernatural can be experienced in daily life and can produce extraordinary effects, for example miracles, cures, messages from the dead and so on. As such, they believe that the normal processes of life, ageing and death can be suspended. They are very pragmatic in that they offer practical	and personal solutions to problems, in particular in helping people to deal with loss. There is no real requirement to believe something if you want to join and no test of membership. The community is rudimentary: the audience at a seance is the typical community.
Reformist *Example: Quakers*	These are often the result of failures of revolutionist and introversionist sects. They follow from the failure of a revolutionist sect to bring about change in the short term and the problem that introversionist sects have in maintaining a community of people, all of whom are concerned primarily with mastery of the	self. The typical reformist sect acts as a social conscience and specializes in doing good deeds. The members aim to be untainted by the wider world because that world is the source of evil and unhappiness whilst doing good. Such sects have an undeveloped idea of God or saviour.
Utopian *Examples: Amish, Mennonites, Shakers, Oneida community*	Utopian sects are more radically opposed to the world than reformist sects, less violent than revolutionist sects, and more interested in social change than conversionist sects. They stress social reconstruction on community lines, where communities are often based on some model from the past. As such, members often oppose or avoid many of the features of the	modern world – cars, televisions, cinema – in pursuit of a simpler, less urban lifestyle. They form religious communities and will not try to convert many people. They have typically developed in the USA as a way of opposing the assimilation of immigrant groups; the community becomes a way of maintaining a distinct way of life.

Source: Wilson (1982)

again in the United States, there are virtually no members of the previously popular Shaker movement.

 Application and evaluation activity

Give two examples of religious movements that have developed sects. Can you think of any political movements that have developed sects?

We will now look briefly at the work of Glock and Stark (1965), who suggest some interesting relationships between religious organizations and politics. They recognize that sects often oppose the status quo and relate, therefore, to people's experience of underprivilege and deprivation. According to Glock and Stark, there are two types of deprivation: absolute, economic deprivation, which tends to favour a political solution; and relative or social deprivation, which favours the development of a religious, sectarian response.

There are two important points about this. First, in practice it may be difficult to distinguish between religious and political responses to underprivilege. As E.P. Thompson (1968) argues, working-class politics developed in Britain within the strongly religious framework of Methodism. There is, therefore, the question of whether the development of politics among the working classes, for example, in nineteenth-century Britain, needed a religious framework (this is discussed in more detail in Chapter 10, pp. 155–7). Second, both religious and political organizations experience sectarian breakaways from the traditional ways of doing things. There are, in fact, many similarities between religious sects and political sects, both in their organization – they are often democratic and egalitarian – and in their beliefs – they reject orthodoxy and often argue that salvation is imminent.

Modernity and the move from church, to sect, to cult

As we saw in Chapter 1, sociology developed in the context of modernity, i.e. complex, industrial, bureaucratic, urban societies. This is also the context for sociological studies of religion. In anticipation of the discussion of NRMs and NAMs in the next chapter, and of secularization in Chapters 6 and 7, we can briefly sketch the process by which religion has been transformed as modernity has developed.

Bruce (1996) provides the best summary of this process when he describes it as a move from **cathedrals** to **cults**. In the fifteenth century in Europe, for example, there was one dominant church and one dominant conception of God. In addition, the idea of individuals with their own wants and desires, who are free to choose what they believe was hardly developed at all. The Reformation of the sixteenth and seventeenth centuries saw the growth of greater religious freedom and a critical attitude towards the role of churches and priests. As modern, industrial society developed in the eighteenth and nineteenth centuries, competing belief systems arose – including scientific ones – and the idea emerged of individuals with the freedom to decide things for themselves. Churches became more like denominations while, at the same time, sects developed which still claimed to have a uniquely legitimate view of the truth and which often represented those who were materially underprivileged. Society now has many different religions and many different gods.

In the twentieth century, with modern, industrial societies becoming more common and more global, beliefs have become much more a matter of individual choice, and 'God' becomes more and more diffuse. NRMs and NAMs have developed, many of which resemble cults. In the context of the more restricted definitions of religion discussed in Chapter 2, many of them look less and less obviously religious.

In the next chapter we will look in detail at this development of cultic movements and what sociologists call the cultic milieu.

Essay question

How useful are the classifications of religious organizations, developed by sociologists, in helping us to understand the wide variety of religious organizations found around the world?

References and further reading

Becker, E. (1932) *Systematic Sociology*, New York: John Wiley.

Bruce, S. (1995) *Religion in Modern Britain*, Oxford: Oxford University Press.

Bruce, S. (1996) *Religion in the Modern World: From cathedrals to cults*, Oxford: Oxford University Press.

Gerth, H. and Mills, C.W. (1948) *From Max Weber: Essays in Sociology*, London: Routledge.

Glock, Y. and Stark, R. (1965) *Religion and Society in Tension*, New York: Rand McNally.

Niebuhr, H.R. (1962) *The Social Sources of Denominationalism*, New York: Meridian.

Runciman, W.G. (1978) *Max Weber: Selections in translation*, Cambridge: Cambridge University Press.

Stark, R. and Bainbridge, W. (1985) *The Future of Religion: Secularisation, revival and cult formation*, Berkeley: University of California Press.

Thompson, E.P. (1968) *The Making of the English Working Class*, Harmondsworth: Penguin.

Troeltsch, E. (1931/1976) *The Social Teachings of the Christian Churches*, Chicago: University of Chicago Press.

Wallis, R. (1976) *The Road to Total Suspicion: A sociological analysis of Scientology*, London: Heinemann.

Wilson, B. (1961) *Sects and Society*, London: Heinemann.

Wilson, B. (1975) *The Noble Savages: The primitive origins of charisma and its contemporary survival*, Berkeley: University of California Press.

Wilson, B. (1982) *Religion in Sociological Perspective*, London: Oxford University Press.

Wolff, K.H. (1964) *The Sociology of Georg Simmel*, New York: Free Press.

Yinger, J.M. (1957) *Religion, Society and the Individual: An introduction to the sociology of religion*, New York: Macmillan.

5 New religious movements and new age movements

Key terms	Key thinkers
New religious movements	Roy Wallis
New age movements	Steve Bruce
World-rejecting sects	Paul Heelas
World-affirming sects	Eileen Barker
World-accommodating sects	
Syncretism	
Cultic milieu	
Millennialism	

Introduction

The classification of religious organizations discussed in Chapter 4 has been very useful in the study of Western religions in the nineteenth and twentieth centuries. However, the work of sociologists such as Roy Wallis indicates that from the 1970s, new forms of religious movement developed which are unlike those discussed earlier. The new forms are now called **new religious movements** (NRMs) and **new age movements** (NAMs). They are often unlike more traditional forms of religious organization in their structure, their beliefs and their appeal.

New forms of religious organization

We saw at the end of the last chapter (pp. 55–6) how Bruce (1996) describes a move away from religion dominated by churches to one dominated by denominations and sects, and then the emergence, in the late twentieth century, of religious movements that have many of the features of cults. These changes have been largely brought about by the development of a more global modern society and a consequent increase in individualism. This is how Giddens (1990) and Waters (1995) define the process:

> The world has become in important respects a single social system, as a result of growing ties of interdependence which now virtually affect everyone. The global system is not just an environment within which particular societies like Britain develop and change. The social, political and economic connections which cross-cut borders between countries decisively condition the fate of those living within each of them. The general term for the increasing interdependence of world society is *globalization*.
>
> (Giddens 1990, p. 520)

> [Globalization is] a social process in which the constraints of geography on social and cultural arrangements recede and in which people become increasingly aware that they are receding.
>
> (Waters 1995, p. 214)

In a global society, individuals not only have a greater choice of things to believe as the beliefs of many cultures become available, but people also are increasingly likely to exercise such choices. These changes have had profound effects on the nature of religious practice, religious belief and how religions are organized.

As we will see (especially in Chapters 6 and 7), this does not mean that established religions have altogether ceased to be important; they may, for example, still play an important role for people who migrate from one society to another, as many Muslim people have done. In addition, the decline in the support for many established religions has not been matched by a corresponding increase in support for NRMs and NAMs. Instead, there is an increasing availability of belief systems from which people can choose, but only some people – and a declining number – choose belief systems that are religious. The idea of being able to 'pick and mix' beliefs is looked at in more detail in Chapter 11, where it is discussed in the context of the development of a postmodern society.

NRMs and NAMs

Sociologists are fascinated with NRMs and NAMs, as are the mass media. For example, 25 per cent of Bruce's book, *Religion in the Modern World* (1996), is devoted to NRMs and NAMs. There have been many sensationalist media reports of religious 'cults' and which claim that cults are, in various ways, dangerous.

Swiss cult offers to clone children

A SWISS-BASED religious cult is launching a company to offer infertile or homosexual couples the chance to have a child cloned from one of them, according to an announcement on the Internet yesterday.

The company, called Valiant Venture Ltd, was launched by the leader of the worldwide Raelian Movement and a group of investors, and will provide a 'Clonaid' service.

Valiant Venture, which expects to have more than a million customers, 'plans to build a laboratory in a country where human cloning is not illegal and will offer its services to wealthy parents worldwide', the undated statement said.

The company would also offer an 'Insuraclone' service, which – for £31,000 – would provide safe storage for cells from a living child or any other 'beloved person', to enable them to be cloned in case of death.

The Raelian Movement, which claims to have some 85,000 members in 85 countries, asserts that life on earth was created in laboratories by aliens known as the Elohim. It was launched in the 1970s by Rael, a Frenchman who says the Elohim contacted him. In a comment accompanying the announcement on the Internet, he said: 'Cloning will enable mankind to reach eternal life'.

The page advertising the company said Clonaid services would be offered at a charge 'as low as $200,000' and would initially subcontract existing laboratories to carry out the cloning operations.

Meanwhile on Saturday, a US bioethics panel recommended that Congress enact legislation to ban the cloning of entire human beings for now, but to allow the cloning of human embryos for private scientific research.

Earlier this year, President Clinton extended a 1994 ban on government-funded human embryo research to include human cloning work.

Source: *The Guardian*, 9 June 1997

Satan's Black Pope joins his master

It was never going to be a normal epitaph, but then Anton Szandor LaVey was not just a run-of-the-mill American Satanist. Jayne Mansfield called him the 'Black Pope' and his followers included Sammy Davis Jr.

His family announced yesterday that the self-proclaimed head of the Church of Satan, who has died aged 67 after a heart attack, would be buried under an epitaph that read simply: 'I only regret the times that I was too nice.'

His daughter, Karla LaVey, a high priestess, admitted her father died on October 29, but said the church had delayed the announcement to avoid upsetting supporters during Halloween, regarded as the leading Satanist holiday.

Sitting beside a life-size waxwork figure of her father with his trademark shaved scalp and flamboyant black cape, Ms LaVey accompanied by her father's long-time partner Blanche Barton, whispered: 'We will follow in his footsteps to keep the Church of Satan alive and strong.'

Ms Barton said: 'No one will take his place.'

A man of eclectic talents, LaVey tried several professions before settling on a religious life. After school he embarked on a career as a lion trainer for a circus, performing in the ring and placing his head in between the lion's jaws. After a near fatal accident when a lion bit his neck, he became a wandering photographer.

But it was through his passion for the 'dark and violent' church organ that he had the idea of founding a church which worshipped Satan in 1966. He achieved notoriety when he performed the first Satanic wedding the following year.

After a cameo as Satan in Roman Polanski's 1968 film *Rosemary's Baby*, LaVey's fame took off, with his books on Satanism selling more than 500,000 copies worldwide.

Source: *The Guardian*, 10 November 1997

The fear of such movements seems to be an important element of popular culture. However, as sociologists, we must be careful not to overemphasize their importance. As we will see later (pp. 63–5), their membership is small and short term; people may join when they are seventeen years old and leave by the age of nineteen. There are many more people who are Anglican, Jewish, Muslim and Hindu than there are who join and follow NRMs. NRMs and NAMs are interesting to sociologists because their proliferation tells us about how people live their lives in – and how they make sense of – complex modern societies.

In this chapter we will look at new religious movements and new age movements, the former dominant in the 1970s, the latter becoming increasingly important in the 1980s and 1990s.

New religious movements

We saw in the last chapter that Wilson (1982) explained the development of a range of religious sects, many of which evolved in reaction to the conservatism of established religions. Wilson's seven-point typology (p. 54) looks at sects that have emerged in Europe and North America. Most of these sects seem to fit with Weber's original idea that sect development is related to forms of material underprivilege (Runciman 1978). It is the materially underprivileged who are most likely to support religious sects. Roy Wallis (1976, 1984), however, identifies new forms of religious movement, many of which are distinctly different from the sects identified by Weber and Wilson. These are what he calls NRMs.

Wallis classifies NRMs into those which **reject** the world, those which **accommodate** to the world, and those which **affirm** the world. This classification developed out of his study of one particular NRM – Scientology.

Scientology

The materials of Scientology comprise the largest written and spoken body of any single philosophic work. Those materials have given rise to the only major religion founded in the twentieth century, and so stand as the spiritual cornerstone for several million adherents across the world. It was additionally through the philosophy of Scientology that L. Ron Hubbard derived his solutions to criminality, drug addiction, illiteracy and social unrest. ... At the heart of [his] discoveries lies a truly startling vision of man as an intrinsically spiritual being who lives, not eighty or so years before death makes us nothing, but, in fact, forever. ... The entirety of Scientology auditing and the training of auditors is delineated by the Scientology Bridge which, in turn, describes a route to ever greater awareness and ability.

(L. Ron Hubbard Personal Public Relations Office UK, 1996, p. 4)

The quotation above is from an introduction to some of the works of the founder of Scientology, L. Ron Hubbard. As we will see, it includes some of the main features of a particular type of NRM: spirituality, philosophies of living, claims to huge membership, cures for social ills, managing death.

The history of Scientology is fairly straightforward. It developed out of a movement called Dianetics, established in the 1950s by Lafayette Ron Hubbard. Hubbard had been a science fiction writer and argued that people could live happier lives if they could get rid of engrams, or traumas, which were the result of past bad experiences. When, for example, children experience rejection it causes them pain; traces of this pain remain in the mind and continue to have effects in adult life. The method used to identify these traumas was the e-meter, which works like a lie detector; it registers electrical changes in the skin.

The e-meter allows an 'auditor' to identify a trauma and, through talking to an auditor about the painful experiences, the 'patient' can be rid of the trauma and its effects. Dianetics was, therefore, a combination of the sorts of things psychotherapists do – encourage people to talk openly and freely, in a safe and comfortable environment, about the problems they have faced – and some religious ideas about the soul, which Hubbard came to regard as immortal.

Partly as a result of hostility from doctors and the Federal Government in the United States – hostility over Hubbard's claim to be offering medical treatment, even though he was not a doctor – and partly to deal with the rapid expansion in the popularity of Dianetics, the movement developed into a religion. This led to the change of name from Dianetics to Scientology and gave the Church of Scientology the same exemption from taxes on income that other religions enjoy in the United States. It is now very popular, as indicated in this extract from a newspaper profile of Scientology.

Cult of Ron beams in from the heavens

JOHN TRAVOLTA says it has changed his life, Tom Cruise claims it helped him to overcome dyslexia and Sharon Stone, Priscilla Presley, Demi Moore and Shirley MacLaine are all devotees.

All right, some Hollywood stars have lifts that stop short of the penthouse, but if the Church of Scientology is not only acceptable but positively trendy in the media capital of the world, why is there so much alarm here about is forth-coming advertisements on British television? Is the controversial Ron Hubbard, founder of the church, still pulling the strings from his celestial abode in the sky?

People pay quite a lot to be Engram-free, and, with a claimed 8m members world-wide (10,000 of whom are supposed to be in the UK), Scientology is big business. Its income has been estimated at £200m a year, with additional assets of £270m.

Source: *The Sunday Times*, 15 September 1996

One of the issues that most interested Wallis was why people become Scientologists. His conclusion was that there is a range of reasons. Some are to do with success in one's job, others with becoming a better person, for example in one's personal relationships. The typical member, according to Wallis, is young, not yet married, just starting on a career or just finishing university, male rather than female, white and middle class. This suggested to Wallis that there was something more to joining this religious movement than forms of material underprivilege; these members were more than likely to be successful but, at the same time, feared the possibility of failing. They experience forms of psychological underprivilege and/or what Glock and Stark (1965) call 'relative deprivation'.

The Church of Scientology became financially very successful and had an internal career structure that made people successful. As individuals became more knowledgeable – more successful as auditors – their position in the church improved and their earning capacity increased. In addition, members claimed that membership *did* make them more successful in their jobs and personal lives.

There is another aspect to the history of the Church of Scientology. As Wilson had suggested, the history of a sect is related to how it deals with the wider world and how that world reacts to the sect. Scientology, in common with many more traditional religious sects, has had a stormy relationship with the wider society. It has had periods of opposition to and withdrawal from the wider society, and periods when it was more open and worked – successfully – to increase recruitment. In its turn, the wider society has at times ignored Scientology and at other times challenged it. In both the UK and Germany, for example, there were attempts in the 1970s and 1980s to make Scientology illegal.

These variations in the relationship between Scientology and the rest of society led Wallis to his classification of NRMs. World-rejecting NRMs (as the name suggests) are typically hostile to the wider society and often receive hostility in return; they closely resemble religious sects. Other NRMs affirm the world; they accept what the wider world says people should do – work hard, be successful in work and personal life – and claim to help members achieve these desired ends. For much of its life,

Scientology has been a world-affirming movement. World-accommodating movements – which in Wallis's work have less importance – are more like religious denominations in that they see that there are many different versions of the truth and regard religion as a largely personal matter. This is how Wallis summarizes his classification of new religious movements:

Figure 5.1 Wallis's classification of NRMs

Source: Wallis (1984)

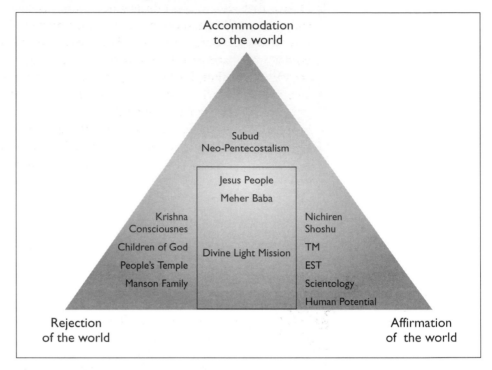

Interpretation and evaluation activity

Using CD-ROMs, books and other sources of data, find examples of one of each of the following sects:

- *world-rejecting;*
- *world-accommodating;*
- *world-accepting.*

Briefly describe their organization and their beliefs.

The world-rejecting movements often have beliefs that are straightforwardly religious. David Koresh, the leader of the Branch-Davidian movement during the Waco siege in 1993, claimed to be a messiah and to have religious inspiration. This contrasts with world-affirming and world-accommodating movements. Scientology, for example, looks less religious than other movements: although Hubbard claims that the soul is immortal, there is no claim to a God and the movement deals with very specific, pragmatic issues including job success. In addition, such movements are often **syncretic** in their beliefs: that is, they combine elements of many belief systems, including combinations of different religions. The Unification Church, for example, combines Christianity and Buddhism, while Scientology combines science and religion.

Joining new religious movements to guarantee success?

Notice that we are again dealing here with how we define religion and what religion actually does. Although many religions have something to say, for example, about what sort of work you should do and how hard you should work, few make the sort of claims that Scientology makes, for instance, to improve an individual's success in personal and work relationships. We will see in Chapter 6 (pp. 150–3) that Weber argued that a certain form of religion – Protestantism – made work a godly activity and urged that *all* legitimate work was good in the eyes of God. However, nowhere did it say that if you believed, joined the church and worked hard, then you would gain salvation. This *is* the claim that many NRMs make: join, learn the truth and success will be yours!

Paul Heelas (1992, 1996) identifies a whole group of people to whom NRMs appeal. He calls such people 'new age professionals'. (We will discuss the idea of the new age later in this chapter, see pp. 65–72.)

> The key to the matter lies in the meanings which are attributed to work. In a broadly similar fashion to the capitalists discussed by Weber ... who did not work merely to become wealthy but treated work as a way to the end of obtaining a 'sign' that they were of the elect, self-religionists ... believe that work caters for something much more important than wealth creation alone. *Essentially work is understood to be a spiritual discipline.*
>
> (Heelas 1992, p. 157)

Many self-religionists – people who regard the self and personal identity as sacred, but also as requiring further improvement and development – work in large corporations where there are high levels of stress and anxiety. The movements to which they are committed do three things: they claim to make large organizations more human; they claim that there are better ways to get the best out of people; they claim that people can always improve. Economic success and something that looks like a religion are thus combined.

The reasons for joining an NRM and the particular type of NRM people actually choose to join will vary. For younger people, who have yet to decide on a career or who are working hard to achieve a career, an NRM that promises future success, as Scientology does, will be appealing. If those same people are failing to achieve what they want and face immense social and parental pressure to succeed, they may join a world-rejecting movement. In both cases, turnover of members is likely to be fairly rapid. Older people who have already made a career may find great appeal in a movement which claims to make work more rewarding, or which makes the hard, rational, grinding world of work more magical.

Magic and mystery

A number of sociologists claim that the modern world is one in which more and more of what we do is governed by rational, scientific criteria; our lives are more and more predictable. For Max Weber (1919/1970, 1904/1974), for example, the modern world is one in which the magical and the mystical have declined in importance. For Norbert Elias and Eric Dunning (1993), the modern world is less exciting. Part of the appeal of NRMs and NAMs may be that many claim to make the world less rational and more magical and mystical. They may reintroduce elements of mystery – flying saucers, ghosts – into people's lives and make a world that is seen as dull and predictable, more exciting.

There is a final dimension to the relationship between the NRM and the wider world.

Eileen Barker and cult-watching

Inform was launched last week as Britain's first objective and officially supported group of cult-watchers. Information Network Focus on Religious Movements promises to conduct research, amass a computerized data bank with world-wide sources, and give out information, advice and counselling in a country-wide network in conjunction with churches and, where appropriate, psychiatrists.

Inform was launched at the London School of Economics, whose formidable guru on new religions, the sociologist, Eileen Barker, had conceived the idea.

'I realized that cults can give rise to a lot of anguish and even tragedy, and objective, value-free science is not going to help if it isn't made available,' Dr Barker said.

Some of the best-known cults like the Moonies, the sexually liberated followers of Bagwan Rajneesh (the man with the fleet of Rolls-Royces who was hounded out of the US by tax men), the Children of God and others have faded from the headlines. Moonies have stopped mass recruiting, Bagwan followers and the Children of God have largely retreated from Europe.

But Scientologists still claim hundreds of recruits a month for their costly, psuedo-scientific self-improvement 'courses' for which students often abandon regular studies. And Dr Barker says hundreds of new, lesser-known or unknown cults are claiming converts and causing, at best, mystification for parents.

Dr Barker interprets cults as the price we pay for a pluralistic society. 'We are bound to get highly dubious efforts to provide one single truth. So much is offered, we don't look at the contract ...'

Now, thanks to Dr Barker's diplomacy, government, churches and academics can act together and settle down to some serious cult-watching and counselling, but with no overtones of cult-bashing.

Source: *The Guardian*, 16 September 1987

'Cult busting' has become a business in which 'deprogrammers' are employed by families and other relatives to 'capture' people back from cults. For sociologists, this raises interesting issues:

● Are people captured by cults in the first place?

● Are they then programmed to believe something entirely alien to what they believed in the past?

That is, how powerful are new religious movements and, if they are not all that powerful, why do people *think* they are powerful?

There is a contrast between popular concern and fear about NRMs, particularly those that are world-rejecting, and the reality of their popularity and hold over people. As Eileen Barker (1984) shows, many NRMs are very bad at keeping members. Only 7 per cent of people who attended an initial workshop with the Unification Church were still affiliated to the church after one year; this fell to 5 per cent after two years and 3.5 per cent after five years. Membership turnover is therefore very high; if people join at the age of seventeen, they are very unlikely to be members by the age of twenty. This contrasts with the public fear of NRMs, that they trap young people, indoctrinate them and keep them captive. This fear then legitimates the work of professional deprogrammers who are employed by parents to 'recapture' their children.

The appeal of NRMs to young people

There is an important link between the fear of NRMs, the changing role of parents and the length of time it takes many young people to attain their career objectives. The period between childhood and adulthood is, in effect, getting longer for many people. For example, more and more people are staying on in education after the age of sixteen, thus delaying their entry into work, marriage and the formation of families. It is during this period that young people are most likely to join NRMs, and parents are most likely to see the movement as capturing their children and breaking up families.

New age movements

The emergence of more and more new age movements (NAMs) – concerned, variously, with dowsing, shamanism, paganism, psychosynthesis, Feng Shui, crystals and so on – is partly historical. The new age is a phenomenon of the 1980s and 1990s; in 1975, there were few shops selling crystals for lifestyle purposes such as health, insight and so on. Now, very many shopping centres and shopping malls have a crystal shop.

Application activity

Go to your local bookshop. If there is a new age section, make a list of the topics covered. What are the major themes of the books in the new age section? How many of these would you call religious?

Shopping for spirituality?

Application and interpretation activity

Search the Internet for evidence of the extent and nature of new age movements. To what extent is the role of the Internet part of what, in Chapter 4, we called cults?

NAMs are also distinct in their organization. Whereas most NRMs are sectarian – that is, they include elements of traditional religions, but those elements are combined in various ways in order to break away from religious and other traditions – NAMs are close to what sociologists call cults (see Chapter 4, pp. 47–9). Most NAMs are either audience cults or client cults. Client cults largely involve an individual relationship between a consumer and a producer: for example, someone selling herbal medicines through an advertisement in a new age magazine. Audience cults are more organized and include the mass distribution of a message through books, websites, the spoken word and so on.

Logging on to a higher plane?

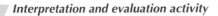

Interpretation and evaluation activity

If you have access to the World Wide Web, find the website of a new age movement. What are its main features? What does it offer members? Are its beliefs religious?

As Bruce (1995) and Heelas (1992, 1996) argue, the new age movement as a whole is extremely broad – it includes paganism as well as practical guides for becoming a better person in the workplace. It is therefore both a fringe and a mainstream phenomenon. It also involves an enormous range of levels of commitment and involvement. On the one hand, there are people who read their horoscopes and believe that they are typical Sagittarians. On the other hand, there are those who were so involved with the Higher Source group that they committed suicide.

Bruce (1995, 1996) argues there are three major themes in the new age movements, which we will now discuss.

New science

The new age is at odds with traditional scientific ways of doing things. Whereas most scientists – on the basis of observation and testing – will reject the existence of flying saucers, or the idea that people can receive messages from the dead, the new age accepts these claims without the need for scientific proof. As Bruce (1995, p. 107) suggests, the supporters of new age movements are most opposed to what they see as the closed-mindedness and authoritarianism of scientists. In addition, the new age tends to see older forms of knowledge and understanding – myths, shamanism, generally how premodern societies did things – as superior to modern forms. These 'old ways' give people a superior way of living in the world and of understanding it.

New ecology

The new age is fundamentally green in two main senses that make it different to mainstream views on the environment: it claims that the planet is an organism, and it links personal problems to environmental ones.

New agers say what more mainstream environmentalists say: that all aspects of the environment are linked, so that everything people do has implications for animals, the climate and so on. New agers go on to argue that the Earth itself is an organism, a living being.

> New agers have taken the system model one step further to suppose that earth is really an animate object – a 'super organism' – that James Lovelock named Gaia, after the Greek Goddess of Earth, which has the rights of a person.
> (Bruce 1996, p. 211)

This view has very practical implications for how many people – and not exclusively new agers – live their lives. For example, we should be vegetarian, we should not kill an animate object, if we do eat meat, then we will damage ourselves, the environment and subsequent generations. As with many new age ideas, living at peace with the environment has become a mainstream idea.

New psychology and spirituality

Hand-in-hand with a belief in the world as an animate object and a rejection of science, there is a great emphasis on the self and the spirit. As Heelas suggests, many of these movements are self-religions: they talk about human potential for self-improvement and give this potential a spiritual content. For example, if someone is trying to become a better person, it is in order to live better with others and to be more attuned with Gaia, rather than simply to be more successful in work; this is, of course, one of the promises that movements like Scientology already make. Self-improvement is central to the new age and makes its appeal very wide indeed.

> The promise is that the Self itself empowers the person as a ... magical producer ... self-help manuals ... hold that affluence results ... [from] contact with one's inner spirituality. Examples are provided by Louise Hay's *The Power is Within You* (1991), Sondra Ray's *How to be Chic, Fabulous and Live Forever* (1990), Ron Dalrymple's *The Inner Manager* (1989) ... Swami Sivananda's *Ways for Success in Life and God-Realisation* (1990) ... such manuals attach little or no importance to 'actually' working to obtain wealth; what is important is getting the God within to do the work.
>
> (Heelas 1996, pp. 66–7)

As sociologists, we need to identify the reasons for the appeal of the new age and to identify those to whom it appeals.

Why the new age?

Remember that for Weber there is a link between underprivilege and support for religious sects. That link is far less clear with NRMs and NAMs, because they appeal to those who are likely to succeed and deal with their concerns about that success and the fear of failure. NAMs seem to appeal to those who already have an affinity for a **cultic milieu** which emphasizes ecology, spirituality, personal growth and a concern that science does not have all the answers. As Bruce argues:

> The social characteristics that predispose some people to take it [the new age] seriously are better thought of, not as pre-existing deficiencies which the innovation remedies, but as conditions for finding innovation plausible. People with no prior experience of introverted self-inspection, no fluency in the language of self-examination, and no confidence in self-expression, find New Age spirituality incomprehensible and hence will not interpret their problems in ways which the New Age addresses.
>
> (Bruce 1995, p. 116)

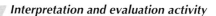

Interpretation and evaluation activity

What is Bruce saying about the sorts of people to whom the new age appeals? Are they, for example, more likely to be teachers and managers than footballers and train drivers? If so, why is this the case?

This suggests that the new age, if it is a religious movement at all, comes close to forms of religion that Durkheim identified as typical of a modern society: 'A free, private, optional religion, fashioned according to one's own needs and *understanding*' (Pickering 1984, p. 96).

The new age does not, in any sense, provide a compensation for problems of underprivilege, either material or psychological. It comprises an enormously diverse set of ways of understanding the relationships between the self and the social and natural worlds, which appeals to particular groups of people. It relates to people's need to understand the particular situations they are in and it allows a wide range of choices as to what people can do and believe.

The new age, the self and narcissism

NAMs clearly offer people a very wide range of beliefs from which to choose. This emphasis on individual choice, as Bruce (1995) argues, is typical of the modern world and something which makes it very different from the world of the fifteenth and sixteenth centuries.

Another important feature of the appeal of NRMs and NAMs is discussed by Christopher Lasch in his book, *The Culture of Narcissism* (1991). They appeal to a concern with the self and how to improve it; people are encouraged to make themselves better, both physically (through exercise) and psychologically (through counselling). Note that many NRMs and NAMs are as close to systems of counselling and psychotherapy as they are to religion.

Who is new age?

Bruce (1996, pp. 219–22) argues that new agers are more likely to be women than men and more likely to be middle class than working class. The strand of the new age that stresses healing and spirituality is especially supported by women. We will discuss the relationship between religion and gender in Chapter 9.

Application and interpretation activity

Design a questionnaire to assess the support for the new age among your relatives, friends and/or peers. Are there, for example, significant gender or age differences in that support?

The impact of the new age

As with NRMs, the numbers involved with the new age and the impact of the movement, as a whole, can be exaggerated. However, we need to look at the issues of numbers and impact in more detail, starting with Bruce's arguments that NAMs have low saliency and low impact (Bruce 1995, pp. 117–23).

An Exegesis seminar

'Exegesis' is an interesting organization. It focuses on self-improvement and runs seminars for which people have to pay to attend. The seminars examine those things claimed to stand in the way of self-improvement, many of which are centred on the individual; for example, a person may lack self-confidence and have a ➤

negative self-image. Seminars combine processes in which the participant is criticized for negative qualities, and processes in which, for example, a better self-image is constructed. The seminars are strictly organized and may include times when basic needs are not satisfied; there may be strict controls on when people can eat, visit the lavatory and so on.

The crystal maze?

There is a great difference between participating in an Exegesis seminar and buying a crystal at a local shopping centre. There is much more commitment involved in the financial and time demands of a seminar than in the purchase of a crystal. However, people who attend Exegesis training and people who buy crystals are both involved with what sociologists call the **cultic milieu**. The cultic milieu is very wide and is made wider by its commercial manifestations – shops, magazines, websites and so on. It encompasses potentially a very large number of people: for example, those who read horoscopes, those who read self-improvement books, and those who are interested in crop circles and lay lines.

Although involvement in the cultic milieu is very wide, relatively few people do things like Exegesis training: more people attend Methodist worship every year than do Exegesis, even allowing for the decline in Methodism. For most people, therefore, NAMs are of low saliency and low impact; they are one choice among many about what to do and believe. Few people order their whole lives in terms of new age 'philosophy'. The social role of the new age combines widespread involvement with relatively little impact.

As Heelas (1996, pp. 90–8) suggests, the new age has become part of the mainstream. It now has two aspects, therefore. First, its *counter-cultural* aspect, which is more world-rejecting and includes an emphasis on ecology, spirituality, mysticism and anti-science (as discussed by Bruce). Second, its *mainstream* aspect, the ideas of which – like the self-religions discussed earlier – can be applied within industry and business.

What does this suggest about involvement with the new age? Heelas (1996) emphasizes that research has not yet been done on the numbers of new agers, assuming that such research is possible with such a diverse group of beliefs and practices. It is clear to him, however, that there is likely to be a range of types of involvement:

> Beginning with the fully-engaged, these are those who devote their lives to the spiritual quest. They are likely to be found working as New Agers, providing healing or running shamanistic events. … The next category of people – the 'serious part-timer' – serves a central role in supporting what is going on. These are people, typically with conventional careers, who turn to workshops and courses on a part-time basis. … Those who incorporate self-spirituality as part of themselves, and by way of part-time involvement, probably amount to a quite large number. Many of the thousands of events put on across Britain are quite expensive and challenging. One assumes that … only the more serious are attracted. As for the less serious – the 'casual part-timer' – these are people who are motivated by their consumerist outlook or to satisfy their curiosity.
>
> (Heelas 1996, pp. 118–23)

Although most religions and, indeed, political movements, attract fully committed followers and those who are less so, the cultic milieu of the new age is distinct: it has a great variety of ideas, it lacks a central organization and it requires only a low level of commitment from believers.

By way of summary, we can say that we now live in a late modern world characterized by an immense variety of beliefs. Although there are churches, denominations, sects and cults, the cultic milieu of the new age *is* new and is, in part, a reflection of the increasing emphasis on tolerance and individual choice. We will see in Chapter 7 (pp. 103–8) the extent to which forms of fundamentalism are reactions to these features of a modern globalized world. The following quotation from Bruce sums up the sociological significance of the new age:

> New Age religion cannot aspire to promote radical and specific change because it does not have the cohesion and discipline of a sect. … But, as has already happened with aspects of its environmentalism and its holistic approach to health, some of its ideas may find themselves stripped of their more esoteric parts and accepted into the cultural mainstream. More important than its immediate impact on the lives of individuals is the part that it plays as symptom and as cause in the erosion of faith in orthodoxies and the authority of professional knowledge. For all its talk of community, the New Age is the embodiment of individualism.
>
> (Bruce 1996, p. 225)

NAMs and the millennium

Millennialism and the end of the twentieth century

Millennialism is the belief that the start of the new millennium (the year 2000) is a time when major social, political and cultural changes are most likely to occur, usually through some supernatural or divine intervention. As we will see below, some millennial beliefs in the supernatural include aliens and space craft. We will see in Chapter 10 that millennialism is much more widespread than the current concern with the year 2000 and that expectations of rapid social change through supernatural means are a feature of many societies experiencing social dislocation and strife (see pp. 157–8).

Source: *The Guardian*,
1 July 1996

It seems that new age ideas are becoming more popular and many of them involve some concept of the end of the old world and the start of the new. This is how Damian Thompson puts it in a study of millennialism:

> The 1990s is a decade bristling with popular theories which combine science fiction, scientific theory and mystical religion. Most, if not all, of them seem heavily influenced by the approach of the year 2000. … The television series *The X-Files*, about a US government conspiracy to hush up a UFO invasion, has been the surprise hit of the 1990s … in America and Europe, the hunger for books and films on esoteric subjects has been matched by a striking increase in near-death experience and alien abductions … Thousands of people [claim] to have been briefly spirited away by extra-terrestrial visitors.
>
> (Thompson 1996, p. 193)

The issue of alien abductions is an interesting one for sociologists of religion. There is a distinct history to this set of beliefs and a common scenario to all claims of alien abduction. Historically, belief in abduction developed in the 1960s and was associated with reports of flying saucers, otherwise known as UFOs. Reports of abductions have, as Thompson states, increased dramatically in the 1990s.

There is a typical account of an abduction. The abductee is most likely to be a woman abducted at night when she is on her own. The abductor comes from a spaceship bathed in light and has an androgynous appearance (i.e., not obviously either male or female). The abductee is then likely to be informed that the aliens are involved in genetic experiments. Where the abductee is a woman, her eggs are harvested; where the abductee is a man, his sperm is taken. The aliens often claim that they can save the human race and give the abductee new knowledge. The abductee is then returned to the place from which he or she was abducted.

The Church of Rael

The belief in abduction is clearly part of a wide cultic milieu in which the supernatural is significant. However, there is now an organized church for those who claim to have been abducted. The Church of Rael has begun to develop a theology based on the idea that the millennium is a time of crisis and that only the church has the means to solve that crisis and move into the new millennium positively.

What, then, is the social context and what are the social implications of the belief in alien abduction? First, the belief looks to the non-sociologist to be ludicrous, yet believers *do* actually believe it has happened. Second, the belief in abduction does contain elements of the new age: changing people's lives for the better, the existence of other forms and ways of life that are superior, a general idea of supernatural forces that play a part in daily life. Third, in common with the historical evidence about the millennium in the year 1000, there seems to be some general concern about how society is working – or, indeed, failing to work. The lessons for the sociologist of religion are, first, that the cultic milieu is extremely wide and, second, that we must be very careful to take seriously what may appear to be very odd beliefs.

Essay question

What are the major differences between new religious movements and new age movements? Do these movements recruit different kinds of followers and, if so, why is this?

Coursework suggestion

There is great interest in new age movements and new religious movements, which suggests an enormous range of possible coursework. For example, you could examine some newspaper and television reports on what the media usually call cults and see how far the reports are sociologically acceptable. You could look at a number of websites of new religious movements and new age movements to see how they attempt to recruit members and maintain their membership. Make a list of products you consider to be new age, and identify retail outlets. Do you consider these outlets to be mainstream? Ask some people who buy new age products why they do so.

You can obtain information on new religious movements from INFORM (Information Network on Religious Movements) at the following e-mail address: inform@lse.ac.uk

DATA RESPONSE QUESTIONS
Item 1

Greens celebrate the natural way of death

Britain's first Day of the Dead was marked yesterday by decorous gatherings in woodland 'natural cemeteries' and an evocation of Diana, Princess of Wales, as posthumous patron of the movement.

The island resting place of the princess's body was claimed as 'what amounts to a woodland burial' by leaders of the green campaign for environmental burial.

Nicholas Albery, editor of the *New Natural Death Handbook,* launched a day of visits to some of Britain's 75 woodland graveyards, by advocating natural burial. 'This is now the fastest-growing environmental movement in the UK,' he said, before launching a display of natural coffins.

'Farmers, wildlife charities and local authorities alike have responded to the demand for alternatives to traditional funerals by setting aside land for woodland burials.'

Participants favour rapidly biodegradable coffins, usually made of cardboard, and are invited to compose their own services, free of the constraints of crematoria and churches. The main open day at the Natural Death Centre in Cricklewood, north London, was joined by site visits to natural burial grounds such as Golden Valley at Swanwick Junction, Derbyshire, where environmentally-conscious dead can be taken to their last resting place by train.

Source: *The Guardian*, 20 April 1998

Item 2

The late 1960s and early 1970s saw a flowering of new cults and sects. Some were Hindu and Buddhist imports from the Orient: Rajneeshism, Transcendental Meditation (TM), the Meher Baba movement, the Divine Light Mission, Krishna Consciousness, and the Healthy-Happy-Holy movement of Yogi Bhajan ... were the best known. Others were psychotherapies that bordered on the religious or which became progressively more spiritual over the decades: Werner Erhard's Erhard Seminar Training ('est') and its spin-offs Psychosynthesis and Insight, Arica, Bioenergetics, Silva Mind Control, Scientology, Kerista, Primal Therapy, Co-Counselling and Rebirthing are examples. All afforded techniques for improving the 'self', but they differed from conventional psychotherapy in asserting its perfectability.

(Bruce 1995, pp. 95–6)

Item 3

Neo-paganism 'a threat to society'

People are increasingly turning to New Age spiritualities and superstition in an eclectic 'pick and mix' approach to religion which could lead to the collapse of our civilisation, warns a church report.

The rise of celebrity astrologer Mystic Meg and the growing interest in psychic phenomena as shown by the cult status of the X-Files television series, as well as in astrology, palmistry and Tarot reading, are all symptoms of the 'fragmentation of belief' which presents the Christian churches with an enormous challenge, the report found.

Bishop Nazir-Ali also warned that the spread of eclectic spirituality was leading to neo-paganism' amongst Christians as believers experimented with liturgy and tried to incorporate a new appreciation of nature into their theology.

A common Judaic-Christian spirituality in Britain has been replaced by a much more plural environment with eastern religions, New Age spiritualities and revived paganism offering a spiritual supermarket. Even Christians were drifting away from orthodoxy by incorporating beliefs from other religions; Catholics were particularly likely to believe in reincarnation, commented the bishop.

The report, The Search for Faith and the Witness of the Church, was prepared over four years by an ecumenical committee representing all the mainstream churches and commissioned by the Church of England and the Council of Churches of Britain and Ireland. It says the 'pick and mix' as individuals insist on working out their own spiritual path and refuse to join an institution helps to explain why 70 per cent of people in Britain say they believe in God but only 14 per cent go to church.

Source: *The Guardian*, 12 November 1996

1 *To what extent is the Natural Death Centre (Item 1) an example of a new age movement?*

2 *What does Bruce (Item 2) see as the major features of the new religious movements of the 1960s and 1970s and what do the names of these movements tell us about them?*

3 *How far is the opposition to neo-paganism by church leaders (Item 3) part of the general opposition to new religious movements and new age movements analysed by sociologists?*

4 *How would sociologists account for the development of, and support for, the movements discussed in Items 1, 2 and 3?*

References and further reading

Barker, E. (1984) *The Making of a Moonie*, Oxford: Blackwell.

Bruce, S. (1995) *Religion in Modern Britain*, Oxford: Oxford University Press.

Bruce, S. (1996) *Religion in the Modern World: From cathedrals to cults*, Oxford: Oxford University Press.

Campbell, C. (1972) 'The cult, the cultic milieu and secularisation', in M. Hill (ed.), *A Sociological Yearbook of Religion*, No. 5, London: SCM Press, pp. 119–36.

Elias, N. and Dunning, E. (1993) *The Quest for Excitement: Sport and leisure in the civilising process*, Oxford: Blackwell.

Giddens, A. (1990) *Consequences of Modernity*. Cambridge: Polity Press.

Glock, Y. and Stark, R. (1965) *Religion and Society in Tension*. New York: Rand McNally.

Heelas, P. (1992) 'The sacralization of the self and new age capitalism', in N. Abercrombie and A. Warde (eds), *Social Change in Contemporary Britain*, Cambridge: Polity Press, pp. 136–66.

Heelas, P. (1996) *The New Age Movement*, Cambridge: Polity Press.

Lasch, C. (1991) *The Culture of Narcissism*, New York: W.W.Norton & Company Ltd.

Pickering, W.S.F. (1984) *Durkheim's Sociology of Religion*, London: Routledge.

Runciman, W.G. (1978) *Max Weber: Selections in translation*, Cambridge: Cambridge University Press.

Thompson, D. (1996) *The End of Time: Faith and fear in the shadow of the millennium*, London: Sinclair Stevenson.

Wallis, R. (1976) *The Road to Total Suspicion: A sociological analysis of Scientology*, London: Heinemann.

Wallis, R. (1984) *The Elementary Forms of the New Religious Life*, London: Routledge.

Wallis, R. (1993) 'Charisma and explanation', in E. Barker, J. Beckford and K. Dobbelaere (eds), *Secularization, Rationalism and Sectarianism: Essays in honour of Bryan R. Wilson*, Oxford: Clarendon Press, pp. 167–80.

Waters, M. (1995) *Globalization*, London: Routledge.

Weber, M. (1922a/1978) 'The social psychology of the world religions', in H. Gerth and C.W. Mills (1948) *From Max Weber: Essays in Sociology*, London: Routledge, pp. 267–301.

Weber, M. (1919/1970) 'Politics as a vocation', in H. Gerth and C.W. Mills (1948), *From Max Weber: Essays in Sociology*, London: Routledge, pp. 77–128.

Weber, M. (1904/1974) *The Protestant Ethic and the Spirit of Capitalism*, London: Unwin.

Weber, M. (1922b/1978) 'The soteriology of the underprivileged', in W.G. Runciman, *Max Weber: Selections in translation*, Cambridge: Cambridge University Press, pp. 174–91.

Wilson, B. (1982) *Religion in Sociological Perspective*, London: Oxford University Press.

6 / A decline in religion?

<table>
<tr><td>Key terms</td><td>Key thinkers</td></tr>
<tr><td>Secularization</td><td>Max Weber</td></tr>
<tr><td>Demystification</td><td>David Martin</td></tr>
<tr><td>Rationality</td><td>Bryan Wilson</td></tr>
<tr><td>Religious surrogates</td><td>Steven Bruce</td></tr>
<tr><td>Specialization</td><td>Malcolm Hamilton</td></tr>
<tr><td>Differentiation</td><td>Larry Shiner</td></tr>
<tr><td>Modernity</td><td>Talcott Parsons</td></tr>
<tr><td>Orientalism</td><td>Rodney Stark and William Bainbridge</td></tr>
<tr><td></td><td>Charles Glock and Rodney Stark</td></tr>
<tr><td></td><td>Grace Davie</td></tr>
</table>

Introduction

Chapters 6 and 7 discuss a debate that has been going on in sociology since the nineteenth century. This debate is about how important religion is in modern societies. As we will see, sociologists have not reached agreement on this issue, even though the founders of sociology generally thought that religion would become less and less socially significant.

We saw in Chapter 2 how many of the founders of sociology claimed that, with the development of complex, modern societies, the social significance of religion would decline: religious practice and belief would become less important in people's daily lives. This process of decline is what sociologists call **secularization**. Religious leaders themselves claim that people are no longer as religious as they used to be; Christian religious leaders are concerned, for example, about a decline in church attendance. As Bruce (1995) argues, there is an increasing number of people who seem to be indifferent to religion, but also an increasing number who see the choice of a religion as one of many choices of belief and lifestyle they make on a regular basis.

Churches will fold for want of a flock

Some of the major Christian denominations are likely to disappear from Britain within a few years as church membership continues its dramatic decline.

Research to be published later this month reveals that membership of all churches in the 1980s and 1990s has plummeted by more than 20 per cent. The Church of England and the Roman Catholic Church suffered a steeper decline of nearly 27 per cent.

Overall membership, 7.5 million in 1980, is expected to fall to 5.9m in 2000.

UK Religious Trends, a comprehensive analysis compiled by Dr Peter Brierley, a former Cabinet Office statistician, predicts that some denominations will die out next century.

The *Observer* reported last month that senior Anglicans and Methodists had held merger talks amid concern over falling numbers.

Dr Brierley describes his findings as 'extremely serious'. He added: 'It looks as though people no longer want to go to church regularly.'

The Catholic Bishops' Conference will meet this week to discuss conducting its own opinion poll. 'We have to find out why numbers are falling,' said a spokesman.

In England, nearly 800,000 people have stopped attending regularly in the past 20 years, a reflection, says the Rt Rev Nigel McCullough, Bishop of Wakefield, of 'the self-centred culture' of the time.

The new figures show both church baptisms and church weddings on the wane. But belief in God and 'spiritual' ideas remains high and institutional Christianity is still showing signs of growth elsewhere in the world.

Source: *The Observer*, 9 November 1997

In recent years, many churches have been sold and used for housing … but churches are also being built.

There is no consensus, however, among sociologists about the causes and consequences of secularization or, indeed, whether secularization has occurred at all. Although most sociologists would probably say secularization has occurred, there are also those who claim that it is not entirely clear.

Before we discuss in detail how sociologists have understood the process of secularization, however, it is important to bear in mind some of the things discussed in Chapters 2 and 3. As we saw in Chapter 2, *defining* religion is problematic, and *how* we define it will influence our views on the process of secularization. As we saw in Chapter 3, *measuring* religion is also difficult, and thus it is not easy to measure its growth or decline.

> [We should criticize] sociologists for assuming that the social presence of religious beliefs [is] evidence that such beliefs have direct and specific social consequences [and] sociologists too frequently examine the articulate and literary beliefs of a dominant class [and see them] as evidence of the existence of a general, dominant ideology.
>
> (Turner 1983, p. 5)

> The supporters of the secularization thesis reply that, on the other hand, there is a danger that religion may be defined so broadly that it can be found behind every bush and under every stone.
>
> (Hamilton 1998, p. 28)

Interpretation and evaluation activity

Look at the definitions of religion discussed in Chapter 2. Are any of them so broad that they fit in with Hamilton's views about finding religion 'behind every bush and under every stone'? What are the main advantages and disadvantages of narrow definitions of religion?

Secularization and modernity

We saw in Chapter 2 how Marx, Weber, Durkheim, Simmel and Freud all argued that the social significance of religion declines with the development of modern societies (see pp. 15–20). In other words, as society grows more complex and more urban; as close-knit communities decline; and as choices about what to believe become ever wider, then religion becomes less significant. This process is described by Shiner (1967) in his analysis of the six meanings of secularization:

- Religious symbols become less important and lose their prestige.
- We regard more and more things as 'this-worldly' rather than supernatural.
- Religion disengages from society and has less to say about how society should operate.
- Ideas about the sacred and the magical decline in significance.
- Rational ways of doing things take over from religious ways.
- Religious beliefs take on non-religious or quasi-religious forms, for example NRMs and NAMs.

Research activity

Look through this book and the introductory sociology textbook you are using to find one example of each of these meanings of secularization.

Talcott Parsons, who was heavily influenced by Durkheim, held similar views about secularization. He suggested that as societies become more complex, institutions become more **specialized** and **differentiated**. As a result, it is harder for religious institutions to maintain their hold on the whole of such a complex society. As Turner (1983) puts it, religion can no longer act as 'social cement'. In essence, religious values and ideas once held in common become less and less significant as society subdivides into distinct groups – social classes, ethnic groups, gender groups, and so on. Because the interests and beliefs of these groups are different, the same religion is unlikely to appeal to all of them. (See Chapters 8 and 9 for further discussion on ethnicity, gender and religion.)

A role play on religion, power and wealth

Divide into two role-playing groups: one group has power and wealth, the other lacks power and wealth.

In your group, develop a religious explanation of its power and wealth, or its lack of them.

*How far could the same **religious** belief system explain both the presence and the absence of power and wealth?*

Sociologists who oppose the secularization thesis argue that an increase in beliefs from which we can choose makes any *particular* choice we make even more significant. Competition between belief systems can increase the vitality of each of them. For individuals or groups that choose religion, therefore, that choice will be socially very significant, particularly as increasing populations mean that there are more people to consume religion (Repstad 1996, p. 3).

As we will see in Chapter 11, the idea that we live in a society where we are free to consume – not only a wide range of commodities, but also a wide range of beliefs – and that the communication of those beliefs is increasingly through electronic means, suggests that we may live in a **postmodern** society. The issue then becomes whether, in such a society, the social significance of religion increases.

The direction of secularization

Sociologists who support the secularization thesis argue that the process goes in one direction only: from societies in which religion is important to societies in which religion declines. Most sociologists would argue, for example, that religion's role – as described by Durkheim – of uniting people into a single community with a common set of beliefs (see Chapter 2, pp. 11–12) is never likely to be re-established. There can be no reversal of this process, any more than there can be a return to a preindustrial society with strong communities and high levels of face-to-face contact between people. We may see periodic increases in religiosity and in the appeal of some religions – for example, on a worldwide basis, Islam has increased its following over the last twenty-five years – but the general trend is downwards. In addition, the *significance* of being religious in the modern world has changed (this is the point of Wallis's and Bruce's studies of NRMs and NAMs, which we looked at in Chapter 5). Religion now has less and less of a public role and is much more about personal lifestyle choices and strategies for self-improvement.

The public and private spheres of life

One of the features of complex, modern societies is the separation of the public sphere – work, politics, the state – from the private sphere – family life in particular. According to Parsons (1951), for example, the public sphere is where we behave instrumentally and ➤

pragmatically, calculating how we can best maximize our wealth and income. The private sphere is where we can behave more emotionally and affectively. This separation also affects religion: whereas state religions, for example, used to have a central role in the operation of the political system, religions have increasingly disengaged from politics and relate more directly to people's private lives. As we will see in Chapters 8 and 11, this disengagement of religion from politics and the economy is characteristic of some religions – many Christian ones, for example – but less characteristic of religions such as Islam.

As opposed to this one-directional view of the process of secularization, Stark and Bainbridge (1985) argue that it is more accurate to describe it as *cyclical*. There are periods in which the significance of religion declines rapidly, but there are also periods in which it revives and increases. They cite the United States, Poland and Ireland as three examples of societies where religion has great importance in the present day. In Poland, for instance, the Roman Catholic church was always one of the main institutions through which people opposed the ruling Communist party, and its significance increased as communism declined in the 1980s.

Views of the past

As Turner (1983) suggests, it is very difficult to decide if the mass of people in Britain and Europe were, in the past, religious. Sociologists who support the secularization thesis (for example, Bruce 1996), as well as historians (for example, Thomas 1973), suggest that the past was more religious than the present. Even though there will always be problems in assessing how religious people were in the fifteenth and sixteenth centuries, for example, Bruce still argues that there is convincing evidence that people were more religious then than they are now:

> It is a simplification, of course, but what one sees in pre-Reformation religious life is a sophisticated, complex organization of formal religion laid over a mass of popular superstition, with the two worlds bridged by the complete and uncritical acceptance of a few simple Christian beliefs. It was universally held that God would judge us and banish us to heaven or to hell as appropriate and that the Church held the key. Only the prayers of the Church, the mediation of the saints, and the re-enactment of the Mass of the sacrifice of Jesus on the Cross would ensure the kingdom of heaven. Ordinary people used the magic of the Church to live their ordinary lives and supported the professionals who performed 'high' religion and acquired religious merit on behalf of the whole community.
>
> (Bruce 1996, p. 3)

Research activity

What, for Bruce, are the main indicators of how religious people were in the past? How should we know?

In contrast, critics of the secularization thesis argue that we can overemphasize the religiosity of people in the past. As Turner (1983) implies, we cannot assume, for example, that because the dominant social class in the fifteenth century regularly attended church and understood the Latin service, that the mass of the population either attended or understood.

Much sociological discussion about the past is concerned with the social context of religious practice and belief, and the availability of alternatives. If the mass of people in the fifteenth century *did* attend church regularly, it could count as evidence *for* the secularization thesis (because more people attended then than they do now), or as evidence *against* it (because the church was the major social institution in most communities and attendance was 'the thing to do': it had little religious significance). If there was a 'golden age' of religion, then we no longer live in that age and secularization can be argued to have occurred; if there was no such golden age, then we may be only a little less religious than our forebears and the process of secularization is of less significance.

The historical evidence does not, however, clinch the argument one way or the other, for two main reasons. First, the evidence itself is simply not comprehensive enough. The further back we go in history, the more sketchy the statistical data become. In addition, we cannot rely on other data – for example, novels, autobiographies and paintings – to supplement the statistical information. Paintings on religious subjects, for instance, may be no more reliable as indicators of religiosity than are data on church attendance. Second, when there is firm evidence for a fall in church attendance, for example, disagreement about secularization only starts up again: those who support the thesis see this evidence as conclusive; those who do not either question the data, or claim that a fall in attendance is only part of the issue, and often go on to point to the importance of the continued significance of religious belief (see Chapter 3), and the growth of religious sects and other new religious movements (see Chapter 5).

Holy Moses! It's the Nine Commandments say vicars

THOU shalt not forget the Ten Commandments. Alas, two-thirds of Britain's vicars already have.

The biblical laws are supposed to be written in stone. However, a random poll of 200 members of the Anglican clergy has found that some could remember only two of the instructions passed down from God to Moses as the basis of the Christian moral code.

The results found that nearly a third (31%) do not believe in the Virgin birth; a fifth (21%) do not believe in the Devil; one in ten (12%) does not believe there will be a second coming of the Messiah, a central tenet of the New Testament; and one in 20 does not believe in miracles, such as healing the blind.

The findings have provoked anger from traditionalists within the church who claim that the clergy no longer preach the text of the Bible and use the pulpit to promote their own political agenda.

Source: *The Sunday Times*, 26 January 1997

Secularization and the West

Those who support the secularization thesis argue that modernity causes the decline in religion, and that modernity itself is becoming more global. Part of this process of globalization involves a decline in the social significance of religion in *all* modern societies, with those that modernized earliest experiencing the most secularization. Although the sociological study of religion developed largely in the context of Britain, Europe and the United States – as we saw in Chapter 4, pp. 43–4, the sociological classification of religious organizations is based mainly on the study of the history of Christian religions – the development of modernity in more and more societies means that the processes which initially occurred there are now much more widespread. In that sense, modernity has become a global phenomenon. This is what sociologists call the globalization of modernity.

Opponents of the secularization thesis argue that religion is still important in the United States, for example (see Chapter 7), and also in some societies that became modern relatively late – for example, the societies of Latin America. David Martin has analysed secularization in Europe and the United States. He also argues that in Latin America, for example, the mass of the population is much more involved with religion than is the case in most European societies, whereas the élite in Latin America are highly secularized. This commitment of the mass of the population includes elements of Roman Catholicism and evangelical Protestantism, which seeks to convert indigenous peoples from their folk religions. Martin says:

> People seem to be able to move easily between the elements of advanced technological culture and another world infiltrated with healings, exorcisms and providential interventions.
>
> (Martin 1996, p. 41)

According to Martin, this process does not seem to be stopping: that is, there is little evidence that, for the mass of the population of Latin America, religious practices and beliefs are in decline.

Orientalism

The Palestinian writer Edward Said (1985) has argued that Western sociologists, philosophers and writers have systematically misunderstood non-Western societies. He calls this process of misunderstanding **Orientalism**. This is how Bryan Turner summarizes Said's views:

> Orientalism … creates typologies within which characters can be distributed: the energetic Occidental (Western) man versus the lascivious Oriental, the rational Westerner versus the unpredictable Oriental. Orientalism … divides the globe unambiguously into Occident and Orient; the latter is essentially strange, exotic and mysterious, but also sensual, irrational and potentially dangerous.
>
> (Turner 1993, p. 31)

In general, Orientalism involves the idea that non-Western societies are inferior to Western ones and lack the means to become modern: they are regarded as backward, rural, unable to appreciate the benefits of science, anti-democratic, and so on. Although this is clearly a distortion of the reality and variety of non-Western societies, it is a powerful stereotype, in that it takes atypical features of the Orient and presents them as typical. The power of this stereotype is shown in Western images of Islamic fundamentalism.

We can apply Said's idea to what sociologists have said about religion. It is an example of Orientalism when Western sociologists argue that all religions will follow the path that Western ones have taken: that is, will all decline in significance. It is also an example of Orientalism when Western sociologists argue that their typologies of religious organizations (see Chapter 4, pp. 43–4) are of universal relevance.

Evaluation activity

Using a variety of sources – including books, CD-ROM encyclopedias and newspapers – identify the extent to which discussions of Islam are Orientalist.

The secularization thesis is, therefore, linked to a wider sociological debate about the globalization of modernity. If sociologists are correct that modernity is now global, then, according to those who support the secularization thesis, religion in all modern societies will show a decline in significance. As Martin argues, however, it is not clear that all modern societies are experiencing a process of secularization.

Secularization, new religious movements and new age movements

What are sociologists to make of the increasing numbers of NRMs and NAMs – particularly in the United States and Western Europe – discussed in Chapter 5? Does this expansion support or contradict the secularization thesis? The answers to these questions are far from clear.

Wilson (1988), Wallis (1976, 1984) and Bruce (1995, 1996) regard the development of NRMs and NAMs as part of the secularization process. As Wilson puts it, 'religion becomes a matter of choice or preference and religious diversity is quite consistent with a secularized society' (Wilson 1988, pp. 207, 208).

The change from a society in which there was one dominant religion to one in which there is an enormous choice of religious belief and practice suggests that secularization has occurred. NRMs and NAMs involve fewer people than churches did in the past, they require less commitment, and membership is often transitory. In addition, their beliefs are often only tenuously religious ones: as we saw in Chapter 5, pp. 60–2, Scientology contains beliefs which are as close to science and psychotherapy as they are to religion. Also, they have a limited social role and no longer operate, as churches did, as centres for whole communities where, for example, people met and were involved in many non-religious activities – gossiping, exchanging the latest news and so on. As Heelas (1996) argues (see Chapter 5, pp. 70–2), such religious movements have **low saliency** and **low impact**.

Opponents of this view stress the argument discussed earlier – about how easy it is to exaggerate the religiosity of the past when large churches were dominant – and also ask how an expansion in the numbers of religious movements can possibly be equated with a *decline* in religion. Stark and Bainbridge (1985) take this argument a little further. They argue that cults develop where churches are weak, whereas sects develop in response to strong churches. Despite the declining significance of many churches, especially Christian ones, the increasing importance of the **cultic milieu** (see Chapter 4, pp. 47–8; and Chapter 5, pp. 60 and 70–2) and the expansion of NRMs and NAMs could be seen as evidence against the secularization thesis. Campbell (1972) develops this line of argument by claiming that although individual cults often have a short lifespan, the cultic milieu is a constant feature of modern societies and has considerable significance for large numbers of people. Using Heelas's view, the cultic milieu could be argued to have both saliency and impact.

Belief and belonging

When we discussed definitions of religion and problems of measurement in Chapters 2 and 3, we examined the importance of both religious belief and religious practice. In Chapter 3, we saw that there is considerable evidence that people *believe* things that are religious, although fewer people than in the past actually *practise* their religion; for example, fewer people now worship in church, and churches themselves are concerned about declining membership. This separation between belief and practice has been used as evidence both for the secularization thesis and as evidence to refute it.

Davie (1994) puts forward three arguments about belief and belonging. First, sociologists have paid too much attention to new religious movements and too little to mainstream religious behaviour. Second, when you look, as a sociologist, at mainstream religion, it is characterized by people who believe religious things but do not belong to a church. This separation of believing and belonging forms part of the process of secularization. Third, however, the picture *is* complex. While it is true that more and more people believe rather than belong, there *are* major variations. For example, there is a rise in various forms of evangelism – committed to converting people to religion – which requires belonging as well as believing (see Chapter 7, pp. 108–10). Also, some groups are more likely to belong than others, for example women and people who live in traditional rural communities. Such wide variations exist throughout Europe, where the UK is less religious than other countries both in terms of belonging *and* believing (see Chapter 3, pp. 35–7).

Winter and Short's (1993) study of Christian religion in Britain suggests, on the other hand, that the idea of believing without belonging is too simplistic as an analysis of the social significance of religion. When they asked interviewees whether, for example, they would seek the help of clergy if they had problems about bereavement or illness, between 60 per cent and 80 per cent said they would. Many of these were people who had no obvious religious affiliation. According to Winter and Short, therefore, the concept of belonging is complex and includes at least three issues: what people believe; whether they belong to a church; and whether they would seek the help or advice of the church even if they were not members or believers. It is clear to Winter and Short that the idea of believing without belonging is too simple and may underestimate religiosity. The large proportion of people likely to seek the help of the clergy indicates that the secularization thesis has been overestimated.

Application activity

Ask your parents and/or friends if they would ask the advice of religious experts about the following:

- *an illness;*
- *a sexual problem;*
- *a problem with a personal relationship;*
- *a problem at work*

What do the answers tell you about the process of secularization and the social significance of religion?

There is, of course, a response to the arguments of Winter and Short. If non-members and non-believers are likely to seek the advice of clergy, they may be doing so in a very secular way: they may also seek the advice of doctors and counsellors and then work out which advice is the most useful. Just as there is a choice of things to believe, so there is also a choice of sources of advice; religious experts, therefore, have to compete with others. We cannot, therefore, assume that when people actually take the advice of clergy they are demonstrating some religious commitment.

Secularization, mysticism and rationality

In the early years of the twentieth century, Max Weber argued that the modern world is dominated by a particular form of **rationality**, which makes social life predictable. As such, the world has been **demystified**.

Weber and types of rationality

According to Weber we can act socially in four ways:

- We can do things because they have always been done. He calls this **traditional action**.

➤

- We can do things because we have some ultimate value for which we strive: for example, building God's kingdom on earth. He calls this **value rational action**.

- We can do things because we are driven by powerful emotions. He calls this **affective action**.

- We can act because we have some particular goal: for example, the efficient running of the economy. He calls this **purposive rational action**.

Although, in today's modern society, all four ways of acting socially are present, purposive rational action is predominant: more and more of what we do is governed by the goal of efficiency, the measurement of quality, and so on.

The modern world has a particular character. Weber claimed that its magical, ecstatic elements have almost disappeared and social life has been stripped of its religious and ethical meaning. We live in a world dominated by purposive rational action, which makes the claims of religion seem idiosyncratic. The world is now demystified. This process of demystification happens *outside* religion (for example, as a result of the rise of science) and *within* religion (for example, the claim by Protestants in the seventeenth century that much religious ritual is a form of idolatry and should be abandoned, see Chapter 10, pp. 150–3).

Science versus religion?

Although, as Steven Bruce argues, science has not caused the decline in religion, it is the scientific way of looking at the natural world that has led to the decline in the magical and ecstatic elements of our lives. A scientific explanation of a natural disaster will, for example, relate it to changes in weather patterns that follow global warming. A religious explanation might explain the same disaster by relating it to how people have behaved: the disaster might be seen as the result of not following God's rules. It is the reference to gods and supernatural forces that forms the essence of the magical and ecstatic aspects of life. It is precisely these elements which science challenges and often replaces. In part, the issue for Weber is whether people find scientific explanations of disasters as socially and psychologically convincing as religious ones.

Those who argue for the secularization thesis support this general view of Weber's. By joining the sorts of world-rejecting sects discussed in Chapters 4 (pp. 46–7 and 53–5) and 5 (pp. 61–3), and by believing in the new age, many people attempt to *remystify* their lives: that is, to recognize the importance of the spiritual and unseen forces, which science often denies.

Large-scale organizations

According to Weber, life in the modern world is often depressing. Weber regards large-scale bureaucratic organizations as formally rational; they allow the sorts of forward planning and levels of predictability required in a complex industrial society. However, such organizations are often not adaptable to the needs of individuals, that is, they are not substantively rational. This distinction is often implicit in how people describe their dealings with large bureaucracies: they see them as faceless, unresponsive, uncaring and so on.

Those who oppose the secularization thesis argue that the large number of new age movements – with their commitment to new forms of spirituality – is a genuine form of remystification which makes the social world less secular (see Chapter 5).

Demystification and remystification

Complete the following table:

Examples of the demystification of religion and the wider society	Examples of the remystification of religion and the wider society
1	
2	
3	
etc.	

Do your examples suggest

(a) a process of secularization?
(b) the continued significance of religion?
(c) neither of these?

We can summarize some of our discussions by taking two examples of the often complex relationships between religion and politics.

Religion and the political

Interpretation and evaluation activity

Can the Rabbi teach us anything of value?

Jonathan Sacks, the Chief Rabbi of the United Hebrew Congregations, is trying to get matters straight. He is *not*, whatever some newspapers may have claimed, a lefty. 'I believe that religious leaders should not take party political sides,' he informed *Telegraph* readers. 'The separation of religion from politics is one of the most important features of a liberal democratic society.'

In practice, this does not appear to mean that the Rabbi, as a religious leader, feels he should separate himself from politics. Far from it. His latest book, *The Politics of Hope*, is, he insists, 'a political work'. It sets out to tell us how 'a certain kind of crisis within Western liberal democracies' might be ' overcome by a new and more effective style of politics'.

The Rabbi's theme, which may sound familiar to those who have previously heard him thinking for the day on Radio 4, or delivering the Reith Lectures in 1990, is the dire legacy of the Enlightenment, in the shape of our excessively individualist, libertarian and relativist society. Britain and America, by his account, lie in a state of almost apocalyptic dreadfulness, or as some philosopher put it in *Juno and the Paycock*, 'the whole world's in a terrible state o' chassis'. To name only a few of its components: rising crime, divorce, illegitimacy, single parenting, Pulp Fiction, adultery, Kurt Cobain, depression, drug abuse, rampant anomie, bad manners, shuttered shop windows, teenage abortion – although not necessarily in that order.

Source: *The Daily Telegraph,* 5 March 1997

Bishops attack 'selfish' Tories

Senior bishops in the Church of England today deliver a stinging rebuke to the Tories for failing to place morality at the heart of government decision making and public policy.

The Rt Rev Richard Harries, Bishop of Oxford, accuses the Tory party of emphasising personal over public morality because 'it wishes to resist the fundamental economic and political changes that threaten the privileged position of its supporters'.

But the trenchant comments of the five bishops' separate New Year messages, published in the *Guardian* today, go beyond criticism of one political party and amount to a comprehensive critique of our political and economic culture.

Taking up the themes of Frances Lawrence, the widow of the murdered Catholic head teacher, who launched a national debate last autumn by calling for a moral renaissance, the bishops insist morality is not just a matter for private individuals and the family but goes to the heart of politics and a government's priorities.

Bishop Harries claims people want a renewal of personal responsibility and a quest for decency 'sickened by so much of what is going on in society'.

Source: *The Guardian*, 1 January 1997

Look at these two excerpts from newspaper articles. Do they indicate that secularization is occurring? Give your reasons.

These political interventions by religious leaders have clearly been difficult for politicians to deal with. They also indicate some difficulties with the secularization thesis. As sociologists, you could use these examples as evidence either to support or reject the thesis. On the one hand, you could argue that it is reasonable for religious leaders to say things about politics and for them *not* to do so is a sign of secularization. That is, for religious leaders to comment on the policies of political parties is an essentially religious activity. On the other hand, you could argue that the claim by politicians that religious people should not intervene in politics is itself evidence for the process of secularization. Although politicians may make this claim because they are unhappy with such religious interventions, their argument is related to what Parsons (1951), for example, argues: religious and political institutions have become more specialized and differentiated from each other.

The religious beliefs of politicians

Interpretation and evaluation activity

Where can Christians put a cross?

I do believe. I don't pretend to understand all of the complex parts of Christian theology but I simply accept it.

John Major

I was brought up a Christian but I was not in any real sense a practising Christian until I went to Oxford. I began to make sense of the world.

Tony Blair

I count myself a Christian, I pray every night but I get uncomfortable when somebody says, 'Are you Protestant or a Roman Catholic?'

Paddy Ashdown

Growing numbers of Labour supporters see the future of politics in Mr Blair's 'ethical socialism'. And while it is hard to imagine John Major visiting a group of capitalist clergymen to explain his theological thinking, the other party leaders have also decided there is a religious vote to be won: they have made their own more modest confessions of piety.

Politics is ripe for religious debate: scores of pressure groups are mobilising religious constituents. Last week the conservative Christian charity Care sent out 100,000 'voter guides' in a 'Make The Cross Count' campaign, urging members to 'vote Christianly', to tackle candidates on euthanasia, abortion and education. The Pro-Life Party will field 50 candidates in seats where no other contender is against abortion.

The election has also begun for other faiths: Muslim leaders have sent mosques a document setting out Islamic principles, stressing the family, race relations and workers' rights. Dr Zaki Badawi, of the Council of Mosques, says there will be no voting instruction, but there is resentment at government failure to support Islamic schools while Christians and Jews are allowed theirs. And last week the *Jewish Chronicle* called Mr Major's comments on Holocaust-denial legislation a sign that 'the battle for the Jewish vote was joined'.

'Religion has a higher profile than at any time during my lifetime,' says the Rt Rev Tom Butler, Bishop of Leicester. 'Religious leaders are being listened to in a way we have not heard before.'

Source: *The Observer*, 23 February 1997

Read the article on the previous page and identify the significance for sociologists of the religious beliefs of politicians. To what extent does the resurgence of religious commitment in the major political parties in Britain refute the secularization thesis?

We will see in Chapter 10 that this issue is made more complicated by evidence that religious convictions played a part in the development of some of the major political parties in Britain and, hence, in processes of social change and social reform.

Conclusion

This has been a very long and complex discussion, and there is no consensus among sociologists. Some support the secularization thesis, others reject it. Still others are relatively undecided. On balance, perhaps we should agree with those who accept that there is a continuing process of secularization as well as processes by which religious belief and practice are still relevant (see Chapters 7 and 9).

We are left with two questions. First, if we argue for the secularization thesis, then *why* did secularization occur? The answer is reasonably straightforward and involves the recognition that the founders of sociology probably got it right; that is, the process through which society becomes more modern also limits the capacity of religious practice and belief to unite large numbers of people and to cement together the various social institutions characteristic of modern society.

No other belief system seems to have replaced religion. It is only when sociologists argue that religion performs some essential function that the idea of religious surrogates – institutions that perform religious functions – becomes an issue for discussion.

Guaranteeing religion

The debate about religious surrogates highlights one of the major problems of functionalism within sociology. If we argue that some functions are essential to the continued existence of society, then there must be some institution to perform those functions. If we then say that any institution that performs a particular function – for example, providing a common set of values – is a religious one, then we are guaranteed to find some sort of religious institution in every society. The definition of what is an essential function and which institution performs it thus guarantees that we will find religion in all societies!

As we saw in the introduction to this chapter on p. 78, it is probably the case that there are now more people who are indifferent to religion than there are those who either actively oppose it or strongly believe something else instead. The combination of the indifference of the many and the strong commitment of the few is, itself, an indicator of secularization.

Our second question, if we accept that secularization is occurring, is this: what are its *consequences*? There are many possible answers, but we will look at two. First, we can follow Weber (1919/1970) and Elias and Dunning (1993) by arguing that modern society is more predictable and rational and that people react by trying to make it more exciting and mystical; this is the motive force behind many NRMs and NAMs. Second, we can argue that as society becomes more complex, the issues that used to be addressed exclusively by religion are now dealt with by a range of different institutions. The enormous growth of psychotherapeutic and other counselling movements deals, in part, with some of the issues which, in the past, were religious ones – why am I unhappy? how can I be more successful? Similarly, it is now medicine rather than religion which seeks to explain why people become ill and die.

Evaluation activity

To what extent does the idea that forms of counselling and medicine now answer some of the fundamental questions that used to be answered by religion indicate that counselling and medicine are religious surrogates?

The secularization thesis: a summary

	In favour	Against and/or not convinced
I Sociologists	Wilson, Bruce, Davie	Hamilton, Martin, Stark and Bainbridge
2 Secularization and modernity	Modernity undermines religion	Postmodernity favours religion
3 Direction of secularization	Secularization as a one-way process	Secularization as cyclical
4 View of the past	Past was very religious	Past not that religious
5 Secularization and the West	Stress on Western societies	Stress on world religions/societies
6 Secularization and NRMs	NRMs as attenuated religions	NRMs as valid religions
7 Belief and belonging	Belief less important if separate from practice	Belief important on its own
8 Secularization and the mystical	Demystification of religion	Remystification of the world

In Chapter 7 we will look at three debates which have led some sociologists to reconsider the conclusion that the secularization thesis has been proved: first, the role of religion in the United States; second, the resurgence of religious fundamentalism; third, the debate between those who argue that all religions should come together – what is called ecumenicalism – and those who argue that each religion should remain distinct and pure – what is called evangelicalism.

Essay questions

Sociologists have found it very difficult to define religion and to measure religious practice and religious belief. Does this mean that they cannot decide whether we now live in a secular society?

*Is the expansion in the significance of new religious movements and new age movements evidence **for** or **against** the secularization thesis?*

References and further reading

Bocock, R. and Thompson, K. (1985) *Religion and Ideology*, Manchester: Manchester University Press and Open University Press.

Bruce, S. (1995) *Religion in Modern Britain*, Oxford: Oxford University Press.

Bruce, S. (1996) *Religion in the Modern World: From cathedrals to cults*, Oxford: Oxford University Press.

Campbell, C. (1972) 'The cult, the cultic milieu and secularisation', in M. Hill (ed.), *A Sociological*

Yearbook of Religion, No. 5, London: SCM Press, pp. 119–36.

Davie, G. (1990a) 'Believing without belonging: is this the future of religion in Britain?', *Social Compass*, 37:4, pp. 451–69.

Davie, G. (1990b) 'An ordinary God: the paradox of religion in contemporary Britain', *British Journal of Sociology*, 41:3, pp. 395–421.

Davie, G. (1994) *Religion in Britain since 1945: Believing without belonging*, Oxford: Blackwell.

Davie, G. (1997) 'The individualisation of British belief', in *Keeping the Faith*, Demos, no. 11, pp. 11–14.

Elias, N. and Dunning, E. (1993) *The Quest for Excitement: Sport and leisure in the civilising process*, Oxford: Blackwell.

Glock, Y. and Stark, R. (1965) *Religion and Society in Tension*, New York: Rand McNally.

Hamilton, M.B. (1995) *The Sociology of Religion*, London: Routledge.

Hamilton, M. (1998) 'Secularisation: now you see it, now you don't', *Sociology Review*, 7:4, pp. 27–31.

Heelas, P. (1996) *The New Age Movement*, Cambridge: Polity Press.

Martin, D. (1967) *The Sociology of English Religion*, London: Routledge.

Martin, D. (1969) *The Religious and the Secular*, London: Heinemann.

Martin, D. (1996) 'Religion, secularisation and post-modernity', in P. Repstad (ed.), *Religion and Modernity: Modes of coexistence*, Oslo: Scandinavian Universities Press, pp. 35–44.

Parsons, T. (1951) *The Social System*, New York: Basic Books.

Repstad, P. (ed.) (1996) *Religion and Modernity: Modes of coexistence*, Oslo: Scandinavian Universities Press.

Said, E. (1985) *Orientalism*, Harmondsworth: Penguin.

Shiner, L. (1967) 'The concept of secularisation in empirical research', *Journal of the Scientific Study of Religion*, vol. 6, pp. 207–20.

Stark, R. and Bainbridge, W. (1985) *The Future of Religion: Secularisation, revival and cult formation*, Berkeley: University of California Press.

Thomas, K. (1973) *Religion and the Decline of Magic*, Harmondsworth: Penguin.

Turner, B. (1983) *Religion and Social Theory*, London: Sage.

Wallis, R. (1976) *The Road to Total Suspicion: A sociological analysis of Scientology*, London: Heinemann.

Wallis, R. (1984) *The Elementary Forms of the New Religious Life*, London: Routledge.

Weber, M. (1919/1970) 'Politics as a vocation', in H. Gerth and C.W. Mills, *From Max Weber: Essays in Sociology* [1948], London: Routledge, pp. 77–128.

Wilson, B. (1966) *Religion in Secular Society*, London: Watts.

Wilson, B. (1988) 'Secularisation: religion in the modern world', in S. Sutherland and P. Clarke (eds), *The World's Religions: The study of religion, traditional and new religions*, London: Routledge, pp. 195–208.

Winter, M. and Short, C. (1993) 'Believing and belonging: religion in rural England', *British Journal of Sociology*, 44:4, pp. 635–51.

The continuing importance of religion

Key terms	Key thinkers
Secularization	Robert Bellah
Fundamentalism	Steve Bruce
Televangelism	Milton Yinger
Christian Right	William Herberg
Ethnic churches	Edward Shils and Michael Young
Civil religion	Chrystal Lane
Evangelism	Ulrich Beck
Ecumenicalism	Benedict Anderson
	Reginald Bibby

Introduction

As we saw in Chapter 6, there is some measure of agreement among sociologists that many religions are in decline and that attendance at many places of worship has fallen in the last forty or fifty years. However, religious beliefs remain important for many people's understanding of the social world. Sociologists argue about the significance of this continuing importance of religion for the **secularization** thesis. There are also other issues in the sociological debate about secularization. They include the following:

● Some religious organizations, even in the more 'secular' countries, have increased their membership and support.

● Some countries seem to have remained more religious than others: for example, the United States.

● Forms of religious fundamentalism have emphasized the importance of strong commitment to religion and to the role that religion ought to play in all aspects of social life.

● There are religious movements that emphasize the importance of evangelism and that aim to extend the significance of a religious way of life, as well as ecumenical movements that try to link different religious traditions.

Sociologists question whether these examples indicate that religious belief and practice still have important social consequences and effects. We will look at each of these examples in turn.

Popular and less popular religions

Some of the statistical evidence presented in Chapter 3 (pp. 30–2) indicates that whereas some religions (for example, Methodism and Anglicanism in Britain) have falling membership and attendance, others (for example, Islam in Britain) are flourishing. When a religion is increasing in significance, for example Islam, there are two questions we need to ask:

● Why is it happening?

● To what extent is it evidence against the secularization thesis?

Support for Islam is increasing: there are more Muslims in Britain than there were in 1950 (see Chapter 3, p. 31); significant numbers of mosques have been built in the last twenty years, while significant numbers of Christian churches have been closed and sold. We will look at the importance of Islam in Britain in more detail in Chapter 8.

Research activity

Identify the religious and secular roles of the religious organizations in your locality. What do your findings tell you about:

● *the importance of religious organizations?*
● *the extent of secularization?*

The major reason for the increase in importance of Islam in Britain is the emigration of Muslims from the Indian subcontinent and parts of Africa during the 1960s and 1970s. Religion became significant for these emigrants, as a means of developing and maintaining community life in a strange new environment. One consequence of this was that the children of immigrants in Britain were encouraged to continue the religious commitment of their parents.

How should sociologists link the growth of religions like Islam in Britain to the sociological debate about secularization? Can we, as it were, trade off the decline in Anglicanism and Methodism against the increase in Islam and say that, on balance, we are about as religious as we ever were? Those who favour the secularization thesis would answer 'no' to this question: while there are special reasons for the increase in importance of Islam, it has occurred during a general decline in religion. As Bruce puts it:

> Only where people still possess a religious worldview are they likely to respond to social dislocation by seeking and being attracted to religious remedies. Cultural defence and cultural transition may keep religion relevant but they will not create a religious society out of a secular one.
>
> (Bruce 1996, p. 125)

According to Bruce, it is only when people look at the world in a religious way in the first place that religion can help them cope with the stresses of migration, for example. As we will see in Chapter 8 (pp. 117–18), any such 'religious worldview' is continually challenged and undermined in a complex, modern society.

Religion in the United States

The latest edition of the *Encyclopedia of American Religions* lists more than 2,100 religious groups, a figure that has almost doubled in 20 years. They range from the most straight-laced form of Judaism and Christianity to UFO cults and the influx of Asian religions.

The statistics yield a portrait full of contradictions. One is that the US is a very religious country. Though nine out of 10 American adults believe that God exists, there is growing disagreement about how God should be described. God is the bearded old man in the Sistine Chapel. God is pure intelligence. God is a goddess. At least eight out of 10 American adults consider themselves to be Christian, but most are hazy about the basic tenets of their faith. The pollsters say that Americans pray more often than they have sex, but no one knows how many consider sex and prayer to be the same thing.

Source: *Utne Reader*, July/August 1998

The role of religion in the United States has been central to the sociological debate about modernity and secularization for a number of reasons. First, the USA is the most modern of societies. Second, it is a society created out of enormous ethnic diversity: indigenous peoples, African, Caribbean, Chinese, English, Irish, Italian, Latin American, Polish, and so on. Third, the constitution of the USA imposes a strict separation between religion and the state: unlike Britain, where the monarch is defender of the Christian faith, in the USA the head of state, the President, is prevented from having such a role. Fourth, the USA is a society in which religion seems to be far more important than it is in Western Europe. Fifth, there has emerged in the USA a strong religious component to political life. Sixth, religious organization in the USA is very modern: for example, many religious groups use television as a major mode of transmission.

Evolution and creation

The importance of religious belief in the USA can be gauged, for example, by attitudes towards Darwin's theory of evolution. The Butler Act forbade the teaching of the theory of evolution in state-funded schools because it contradicted the account of creation given in the Christian Bible. The Act was not repealed until 1967. Even now, in many states, evolution can only be taught as a theory, not as accurate empirical fact. For many people, religion takes precedence over science and the biblical account of creation is believed to be literally true.

What do all these things tell us about the social significance of religion? How might they affect our views on the secularization thesis? We will examine three issues:

● The importance of 'televangelism'.

● The debate about the political importance, or otherwise, of the Christian Right in American politics.

● The development of what Yinger (1957), Bellah (1970, 1975) and others have called 'civic' or 'civil religion'.

Televangelism

The mass media have become a very important part of religion in the USA. This importance goes far beyond the kind of media religion found in the UK, such as the daily service on radio and Sunday services on television. A good example is Pat Robertson's Christian Broadcasting Network (CBN) (see Bruce 1990, ch. 3). CBN uses satellite and cable technology to broadcast its programmes into American homes, 24 hours a day. CBN's funding derives partly from its viewers (who provide credit card donations) and partly from the sale of advertising space on its network.

CBN offers much more than religious services. For example, it offers counselling to people on a range of problems. Once someone has made a donation, the network will send them direct mailshots as well as a letter of thanks, which, through the use of advanced word-processing software, can be made to appear personal and individual. All information on those who donate money is computerized and regularly updated.

The churches that organize this kind of **televangelism** also offer services outside the mass media. The evangelist Oral Roberts has established a university. The Thomas Road Baptist Church established by Jerry Falwell runs a nursing home and adoption service for unmarried mothers and has plans for a retirement home for older church members. Its Liberty University has a wide range of Faculties and the church trains people to evangelize, that is, to convert people to the truth of its religion.

Generally, the message of the religious broadcasting networks is conservative and includes elements of what sociologists call **fundamentalism**; in particular, the idea that the Christian Bible is both literally true and a guide to how to live one's daily life. This tends also to include a range of ethical and political messages, such as an anti-abortion stance and the view that 'too much government' is bad.

Sociologists debate the effects of televangelism. Is there really a large body of conservative Christians in the USA which televangelism serves, or is televangelism itself producing a large number of conservative Christians? Bruce concludes:

> For all that the audience for religious television is quite large (perhaps 8 per cent of the total viewing population), watching religious television pro-grammes is still an infrequent activity of a small part of the American people … not much televangelism is consumed by not many people. Even fewer actually give financial support. Televangelism exists because there is a large conservative Protestant milieu; not the other way around.
>
> (Bruce 1990, pp. 233–4)

The debate about televangelism raises two important issues. The first is that sociologists can easily overestimate the importance of televangelism simply because they tend also to overemphasize the importance of the mass media in general. A lot of media sociology developed out of the fear that one of the effects of mass media might be to manipulate people.

The manipulative view of the mass media

The fear that the mass media may possess the power to manipulate people has its origins in the way that the Nazi party in Germany during the 1930s and 1940s influenced people via the press and radio broadcasting. The major problem with all theories about the manipulative power of the mass media is that audiences are assumed to comprise isolated individuals, whereas in reality they comprise different groups of people who analyse the information they receive and may, therefore, be very difficult to manipulate. In addition, such views imply that the audience is not sufficiently intelligent or aware to evaluate what is being said.

Second, sociologists can easily miss some of the most interesting features of televangelism, in particular the way that it duplicates many of the structures and strategies of non-religious organizations – advertising, direct mail, large-scale bureaucracies, and so on. The large organizations typical of modern industrial societies provide the framework for the messages of the televangelists themselves. In effect, religions in the USA – and to a lesser extent in Britain and Western Europe – have increasingly become businesses.

And the church saw that business was good

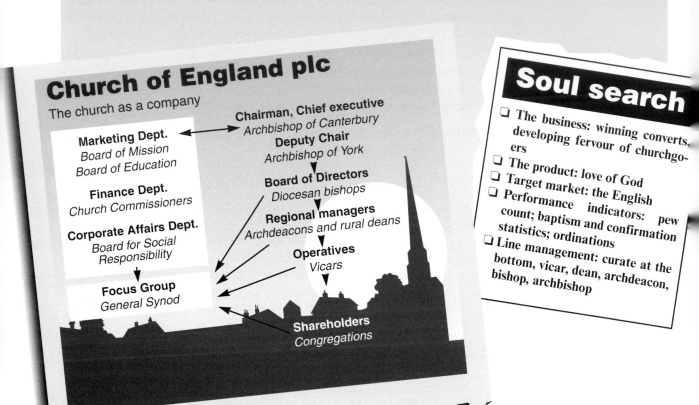

Church of England plc
The church as a company

Chairman, Chief executive
Archbishop of Canterbury
Deputy Chair
Archbishop of York

Marketing Dept.
Board of Mission
Board of Education

Finance Dept.
Church Commissioners

Corporate Affairs Dept.
Board for Social Responsibility

Focus Group
General Synod

Board of Directors
Diocesan bishops

Regional managers
Archdeacons and rural deans

Operatives
Vicars

Shareholders
Congregations

Soul search
- The business: winning converts, developing fervour of churchgoers
- The product: love of God
- Target market: the English
- Performance indicators: pew count; baptism and confirmation statistics; ordinations
- Line management: curate at the bottom, vicar, dean, archdeacon, bishop, archbishop

Source: *The Guardian*, 18 October 1997

The Christian Right

We have already seen that many of the religious networks in the USA are politically right-wing and conservative – anti-abortion, anti-unmarried mothers, anti-Federal government, pro-Republican, pro-family. However, the extent of their political influence is questionable. Does Bruce's (1990) view that televangelism exists because there is already a conservative milieu apply to the political influence of the **Christian Right**?

The answer to this question is, in fact, fairly simple. Members of the Christian Right are in a minority. Although many of them have ideas in common – support for the traditional family, for example – they are divided by region, education, occupation and so on. They do not form a coherent group with common political aspirations. Indeed, as Bruce (1990) shows, many people who watch religious broadcasts do not approve of televangelists attempting to gain political office. Although they may be intensely religious, many viewers still seem to accept the constitutional separation of religion and state. There is, therefore, no coherent political movement: most people who watch religious television do so in their own homes, regard religion as a family matter, and do not take their religion into their work lives or their politics. This channelling of religion into the private sphere may in itself be a sign of secularization.

Civil religion

According to Herberg (1983), the most important influence on religion in the USA is the enormous range of religious traditions brought to the country by migrants from around the world. What Herberg calls **ethnic churches** – for example, the variety of different religious organizations serving Protestants from Sweden, Germany, Britain and so on – enabled first-generation migrants to cope with their migrant status and the process of becoming American citizens. In subsequent generations, ethnic churches became less important; instead, religion in a general, non-denominational sense became more important. The title of Herberg's (1983) book – *Protestant, Catholic, Jew* – indicates the point he makes: to not be religious is to not be American. Part of the USA's cultural and political milieu requires that 'being American' also entails being part of a common religious culture. This does not necessarily mean participating in religious worship, nor having strong religious convictions.

This idea of a general religious milieu – a vague religious background to social life – is taken up by Bellah and others in a discussion of what they call civic or **civil religion**. Bellah (1970), studying Britain and the USA, Shils and Young (1953), studying the British coronation, and Lane (1981), studying the former Soviet Union, all argue that civil religions are important.

Defining civil religion

Civil religion is a set of secular symbols and rituals that provide some of the sense of belonging, social solidarity, and awe usually associated with religion and the sacred. … Until recently, the importance of Lenin's tomb in Moscow was a clear reflection of the power of civil religion. In similar ways, in the United States, heroic figures such as George Washington and Abraham Lincoln have assumed a mythic significance with the power to generate a measure of social cohesion even in a society that is full of ethnic and racial diversity.

(Johnson 1995, p. 36)

For Bellah (1970), the kinds of sacred symbols described by Johnson (1995) provide solidarity and coherence to a society of very diverse cultures and origins. It is their sacred significance that makes these symbols resemble and perform the functions of religions. Bellah argues, however, that even these civil religions are in decline:

[There is the] erosion of common moral and religious understanding ... a tendency to rank personal gratification above obligation to others correlates with a deepening cynicism about the established social, economic, and political institutions of society.

(Bellah 1975, p. x)

Martin Luther King's birthday is celebrated as a national holiday in the USA.

Whereas Bellah initially viewed civil religions as providing the sorts of cohesion previously provided by traditional religions, he came to argue that they are less and less able to do this. Bellah does not mention the potential for civil religion to divide people along ethnic and racial lines. Many sacred figures – presidents, for example – are white, male and Protestant. Other sacred figures – Martin Luther King, for example – provide a role model for some people and not others.

Shils and Young (1953) argue that rituals surrounding the British monarchy – in their study of the coronation of Elizabeth II – are also instances of civil religion. The coronation did much more than simply take place in a religious building and symbolize the relationship between the monarch and the Church of England. It also signified national unity: as a ritual watched and listened to by many, it produced feelings of unity in people, many of whom were not religious. In addition, many of those who were religious were not Christian. Rituals of monarchy are civil religions which, as with Bellah's examples, produce social solidarity in a potentially divided society.

The coronation of Queen Elizabeth II: an instance of civil religion?

A friend for life to the sick and hurting

Mass pilgrimage on the trains

Through the long night the capital becomes a shrine

The making of the myth of Saint Diana

A new divine cult starts here

Research and evaluation activity

To what extent was the funeral of Diana, Princess of Wales, a form of civil religion?

How does all that we have discussed so far about religion in the USA and about civil religion relate to the secularization debate? On balance, it would seem that televangelism is a minority interest and that religious belief in the USA has been slimmed down to simply being the sign of a good citizen. If we agree with Herberg, Bellah and Bruce, then religion in the USA does not invalidate the secularization thesis. Indeed, the entry of religion into the market-place for beliefs, its use of modern media and computer technology, and its adoption of business methods, may indicate the secularization of religion itself.

Religious and other fundamentalisms

Sociologists have become interested in the development of religious **fundamentalism**. Religious fundamentalism is a form of religious practice and belief which argues that we need to return to a time when religion was more important, had a role to play in daily life, and provided definitive answers to moral problems and questions of right and wrong.

Back to fundamentals

The term 'fundamentalism' has been applied to Islam since 1957, when the phrase surfaced in the Middle East Journal. But the first mainstream use occurred in the *Observer* on September 27 1981. In an article which compared the Koran to Mein Kampf, Anthony Burgess talked of 'the phenomenon of the new, or rather very old, Islam, the dangerous fundamentalism revived by the ayatollahs and their admirers as a device, indistinguishable from a weapon, for running a modern state'. The article was widely referred to, and soon other commentators and publications were linking 'Islamic' and 'fundamentalist'.

Many Muslims object that the phrase misleadingly implies that the Koran sanctions political extremism. They point out that the word 'fundamentalism', coined by American Protestants after the Civil War, originally implied a re-affirmation of the 'fundamentals' of Christian theology and interpretation of scriptures: in particular, it insisted on a literal interpretation of the Bible. Yet the extremism Burgess and others refer to is about politics, not theology.

Source: *The Guardian*, 20 October 1997

Stereotyping fundamentalism

There is a powerful popular image of fundamentalism contained, for example, in mass-media portrayals of Islamic fundamentalism in general, and particularly Islamic fundamentalism in Iran. The elements of this stereotype are easily identifiable: fundamentalists are fanatical, violent, anti-democratic and exist outside the modern world; fundamentalism is dangerous because, as in the Salman Rushdie affair, it claims to have jurisdiction outside the countries in which it exists. This stereotype of fundamentalism is, as we will see below, inaccurate. It is an example of how Western people think about and conceptualize other cultures; that is, an example of Orientalism (see Chapter 6, pp. 84–5).

In reality, the potential for fundamentalism exists in most, if not all, religions, and also forms a part of many political movements. Fundamentalism is not – as popular images often seem to assert – restricted to premodern societies. Indeed, as Davie (1995) argues, fundamentalism is a *modern* phenomenon:

> Two crucial points appear immediately: the existence of essential truths and their application to twentieth century realities. Both elements need to be present, for the word fundamentalism should not normally be used to describe the traditional elements of religion that have been left undisturbed by the modern world, nor does it mean the creation of new ideas. It evokes, in contrast, the reaffirmation of essential truths within a situation that has been profoundly disturbed by the pressure of an expanding global economy and the effects that this has had on social, political or ideological life.
>
> (Davie 1995, pp. 2–3)

Research and evaluation activity

Identify one fundamentalist religious movement and one fundamentalist political movement. What are their main features?

Fundamentalist movements have many things in common. They:

- call for a return to tradition in the face of the power of modernity to destroy tradition;
- call for a return to certainty in the face of relativism and uncertainty;
- call for a return to community in the face of the collapse of communities;
- often call for the sanctification of politics;
- often believe in the immediate prospect of radical change which will deliver these things;
- tend to be characterized by high levels of engagement, and members seem, generally, to be more committed and fervent than those, for example, who support mainstream political parties.

Return to tradition

Fundamentalists believe that the destruction of traditional ways of doing things – in particular, the decline in religion and religious values – has led to a range of social problems, including selfishness, addictions of one form or another, violence and educational failure. The solution to these problems is a return to traditional ways of doing things: in Britain, such a return to tradition is often labelled a return to Victorian values.

It is obvious to sociologists, of course, that traditional values themselves are problematical. The Victorian standard of sexual morality was, for example, more repressive for women than for men. In addition, it is far from clear that the image that fundamentalists have of the past is really accurate (see below, p. 106).

Inventing tradition

Members of fundamentalist movements often spend time replaying their history in the present day. For example, Afrikaners, the descendants of white, Dutch settlers in South Africa, re-enact significant historical events – such as battles or political victories – that happened in the eighteenth and nineteenth centuries. They are, in that sense, inventing a tradition and using it to draw attention to how they feel that the present way of doing things – in the case of South Africa, political rule by a black majority – is wrong. We will look at the role of significant historical events and how people celebrate them in Chapter 8, when we study religion in Northern Ireland.

Return to certainty

Relativism characterizes much of our lives. As individualism increases, we have more choices about what we should do. There are fewer simple answers to problems and no agreed answers to questions such as 'Is abortion acceptable?', 'Is the family still important?', 'How should I discipline my children?' Part of the fundamentalist's desire to return to traditional ways of doing things is to return to certainty. In some cases, that certainty is based upon religious belief: the Christian Right in the USA opposing abortion; and Hindu fundamentalists in India attaining political office by arguing for a return to the certainties of Hindu faith.

As the modern world becomes more global, national and local issues seem to get lost, so some of the sources of certainty – the possibility of endless economic growth, the value of science, for example – are themselves criticized. As Beck (1992) and other sociologists have argued, we increasingly live in a risk society, where the degree of risk and danger that people feel has dramatically increased. Fundamentalism can provide certainty in the face of greater risk and uncertainty.

Return to community

The reasons for the lack of certainty felt in the modern world are partly located by fundamentalists in the collapse of communities in which individuals have face-to-face contact with a small number of people. Fundamentalists assert that only by returning to such communities will tradition and certainty be re-established and problems associated with the anonymity of modern life – for example, crime and violence – be solved.

As Benedict Anderson (1983) suggests, such communities are imaginary. They are based on myths about the past – for example, that community life really was better – and forms of nostalgia. What is often forgotten in this myth of the past is that community life – for example, in sixteenth-century Britain – was often dangerous, with high death rates and little privacy.

The sanctification of politics

Islamic fundamentalism in Iran and Christian fundamentalism in the USA both argue that religion should play a central role in politics; religious values should inform political decisions and how the state itself should operate. As Bruce (1990) and Davie

(1995) suggest, it is doubtful that this has actually happened in the USA. The case of Iran is slightly more complicated. Religious law, for example, does influence how people live their daily lives and does affect political decisions. However, despite religious injunctions against usury — that is, charging interest when lending money — there is a stock exchange in the Iranian capital of Tehran which is part of the global money and shares market.

This relates to our discussion of religious sects in Chapters 4 and 5. How can a sect maintain the purity of its message when it has to deal with the world around it? This question can also be asked of large-scale state religions (for example, Islam in Iran) and political movements (for example, communist parties in developing countries). An organization can adopt two possible strategies: either remain true to the original message and therefore limit potential support, or modify the message and increase support. Both these strategies have the potential for sectarian splits within the movement: often, those who want to adhere to the original message separate from those who argue for compromise.

The immediate prospect of radical change

It is a characteristic of some fundamentalist movements to link the return to tradition, certainty and community to some imminent, radical transformation of society in which adherents will play a central role. We will look at this in Chapter 10.

High levels of engagement and committed members

A fundamentalist movement tends to have high levels of engagement. Generally, members seem to be more committed and fervent than those who support mainstream movements. This is a result of the movement's certainty about its message and the frequent desire to convert others.

Fervent support for fundamentalist movements becomes part of their negative portrayal in the mass media. For example, it is part of the media portrayal of Islamic fundamentalism discussed on pp. 104–5 and also part of media attitudes towards such groups as animal rights campaigners.

The challenge of fundamentalism

Explaining fundamentalism is a particular challenge to sociologists. This is how Davie describes the issues:

> The study of fundamentalism demands very particular skills on the part of the sociologist. It requires, first of all, a sense of understanding and empathy: what does it feel like to be in a situation in which patterns of belief and practice established for centuries are under attack? It expects, in addition, considerable sensitivity to world views other than the sociologist's own. It is an area of sociological study in which a little knowledge of other world faiths can at times be a dangerous thing.
>
> (Davie 1995, p. 3)

Sociologists must try to be relativists when they approach other people's ways of life: they must look at how other societies work in the context of those societies themselves.

The balance of the sociological argument seems to be that fundamentalist movements are responses to the changes that modernity has brought about – relativism, individualism, bureaucracy and so on. As such, they are more *responses* to secularization than they are proof that the process of secularization is not occurring.

Evangelism and ecumenicalism

Liberal bishop blocked

Evangelists fighting homosexuality in the Church of England have derailed attempts to place one of Britain's most respected bishops in the key diocese of Southwark.

Evangelists in Southwark want a bishop who would gradually push homosexuals out. 'Out of 500 clergy in Southwark there are about 150 who are either actively homosexual or supportive of gays,' Mr Balfour said. 'We're not looking for a witch-hunt but the new bishop has got to have a policy of stopping gays coming into the diocese and gradually replace those already here with people who take an orthodox view. It will take about 20 years.'

Southwark has always been controversial. In November 1996 the area's evangelists were outraged when the Cathedral hosted a service celebrating 20 years of the Gay and Lesbian Christian movement, which was attended by more than 2,000 people.

Source: *The Guardian*, 7 March 1998

Liberal Catholics dismayed by papal edict

Liberal Catholics responded with incredulity and dismay yesterday to the Pope's edict to stamp out dissent.

Pope John Paul II has ruled in an apostolic letter that on a wide range of issues, including women as priests, the Vatican's teaching is to be regarded as infallible and binding on all Catholics, or they will face punishment ranging from warnings to excommunication.

What particularly angers liberal Catholics is that Cardinal Joseph Ratzinger, head of the Congregation for the Doctrine of the Faith, in his explanatory note to the Pope's Letter specifically ruled out debate on women priests. 'There is no basis in scripture to limit the priesthood to men only,' said Mike Hiland, a married Catholic priest and co-ordinator of the Advent group.

Source: *The Gardian*, 3 July 1998

Churches join forces to lead crusade into the millennium

The Archbishop of Canterbury, Cardinal Basil Hume and the Chief Rabbi, Dr Jonathan Sacks, have sealed a historic pact to promote 1999 as a year of national reflection on moral values.

In a further radical move, the three are also to open talks with leaders of Britain's Muslim, Sikh and Hindu communities to create a broad-based coalition examining the shared values we will live by in the twenty-first century.

In another development the Churches Together's Prayer and Millennium Group has christened the year 'A Chance To Start Again' and recruited the award-winning design consultant Martin Lambie-Nairn to come up with ideas to catch the public's imagination.

Source: *The Observer*, 18 May 1997

Research activity

What are the main features of those religions which are evangelical and those which are not?

Many religions try to convert people to their system of belief, that is, to evangelize. Both Islam and some forms of Christianity are or have been evangelical. However, there are also processes by which people from different religious traditions try to come together; this is what is meant by **ecumenicalism**. This distinction between evangelism and ecumenicalism can be related to the discussion of religious organization in Chapter 4. The form of religious organization which sociologists identify as the **church** (see pp. 45–6) tends to claim a monopoly of the truth. As such, it is likely to have a relatively hostile or distant attitude to other religious organizations and may, as a consequence, seek to evangelize. Denominations, on the other hand, recognize that there are various religious traditions, all of which have something to offer; this suggests an ecumenical stance.

A number of sociologists, including Bibby (1974, 1990) and Bruce (1990), have discussed the significance of evangelism and ecumenicalism in the context of religious organizations and how they relate to the wider social world. Their general argument is quite straightforward: as more and more religious organizations take on a denominational form, evangelical movements become more socially significant. This is, in fact, a simplification of what happens, for a number of reasons. Evangelical movements in a wide variety of countries – Australia, the USA, Scotland, Latin America – have tended to maintain their congregations, while the congregations of more denominational organizations have declined. Processes of recruitment to evangelical organizations are distinct: members come from among those who are already religious, many of whom reject the more liberal and open-minded views of denominations. Only a small proportion – less than 25 per cent – are converts. Most converts are the children of those who are already evangelicals.

In general terms, evangelicals appear to form a greater proportion of those who are religious only because all other religions are in decline. In that sense, evangelism is close to those movements we have called fundamentalist, in as much as they represent a reaction to the role of religion in a complex global society.

Ecumenicalism represents the dominant trend in religious organizations towards a denominational form.

Conclusion

Chapters 6 and 7 have both assessed the secularization thesis. Although religion continues to be important in many societies – the USA, and in many countries in Latin America, for example – there have been significant changes in how religion is practised, in the nature and effects of religious beliefs and in the social significance of religion. Many sociologists would call these changes *secularization* and argue that religion is still important, but within a predominantly secular society. We can indicate the extent of these changes with a final example:

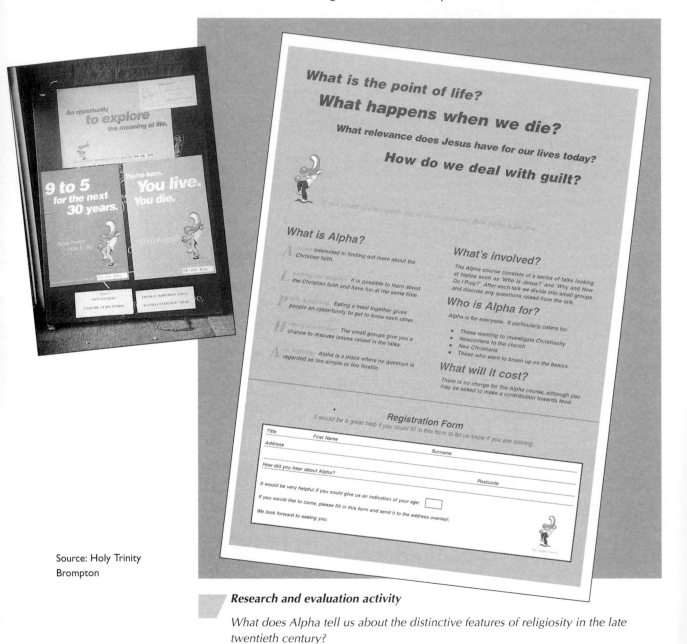

Source: Holy Trinity Brompton

Research and evaluation activity

What does Alpha tell us about the distinctive features of religiosity in the late twentieth century?

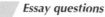

Essay questions

Is the importance of fundamentalism a basis for arguing that the process of secularization has been exaggerated?

References and further reading

Anderson, B. (1983) *Imagined Communities*, London: Verso.

Beck, U. (1992) *Risk Society*, London: Sage.

Bellah, R. (1970) 'Civil religion in America', in *Beyond Belief: Essays in religion in a post-traditional world*, New York: Harper and Row, pp. 168–89.

Bellah, R. (1975) *The Broken Covenant: American civil religion in a time of trial*, New York: Seabury Press.

Bibby, R. (1974) 'Sources of religious involvement', *Review of Religious Research*, 15:71–9.

Bibby, R. (1990) *Fragmented Gods*, Toronto: Stoddart.

Bocock, R. and Thompson, K. (1985) *Religion and Ideology*, Manchester: Manchester University Press and Open University Press.

Bruce, S. (1990) *Pray TV: Televangelism in America*, London: Routledge.

Bruce, S. (1995) *Religion in Modern Britain*, Oxford: Oxford University Press.

Bruce, S. (1996) *Religion in the Modern World: From cathedrals to cults*, Oxford: Oxford University Press.

Chaney, D. (1983) 'The symbolic mirror of ourselves: civic ritual in mass society', *Media, Culture and Society*, 5:2, pp. 119–35.

Davie, G. (1995) 'Competing fundamentalisms', *Sociology Review*, 4:4, pp. 2–7.

Davie, G. (1997) 'The individualisation of British belief', in *Keeping the Faith*, Demos, no. 11, pp. 11–14.

Hamilton, M.B. (1995) *The Sociology of Religion*, London: Routledge.

Herberg, W. (1983) *Protestant, Catholic, Jew: An essay in American Religious Sociology*, New York: Doubleday.

Johnson, A.G. (1995) *A Blackwell Dictionary of Sociology*, Oxford: Blackwell.

Lane, C. (1981) *Rites of Rulers: Ritual in industrial society, the Soviet case*, Cambridge: Cambridge University Press.

Shils, E. and Young, M. (1953) 'The meaning of the Coronation', *Sociological Review*, 1:2, pp. 63–82.

Yinger, J.M. (1957) *Religion, Society and the Individual: An introduction to the sociology of religion*, New York: Macmillan.

8 Religion, ethnicity and ethnic identity

Key terms	Key thinkers
Ethnicity	Ken Pryce
Ethnic identity	Richard Jenkins
Ethnic group	Tariq Modood
Ethnic minority group	Richard Berthoud
Migration	Steve Bruce
Cultural identity	Robert Ash
Assimilation/assimilationism	Ian Goodchild
	Grace Davie

Introduction

In Chapter 7, we looked at the role religion has played in the United States; in particular, how the religions of different ethnic groups have been essential to help people cope with **migration** and adjustment to a new society (see pp. 101–2). This chapter will focus on some important relationships between religion and **ethnicity**: the role of religion among people of Asian and Afro-Caribbean origin in Britain, and religion in Northern Ireland. We will note the great diversity of ethnic groups in Britain and the significance of religious affiliation for those various ethnic groups.

Ethnicity and ethnic groups

Ethnicity

Sociologists use a variety of terms to discuss ethnicity, among them
- ethnic group;
- ethnic minority group;
- minority ethnic group.

These terms will occur frequently in your reading and are often used to describe the same thing: groups that are culturally identifiable and distinct from others. In this chapter, we will use **ethnic group** to refer to groups that are culturally distinct and **ethnic minority group** where such groups are numerically and/or politically and culturally in a minority.

We need to be clear about exactly what we mean by 'ethnicity' and 'ethnic group':

> An ethnic group [is] defined as a *community* whose *heritage* offers important characteristics in common between its members and which makes them distinct from other communities. There is a boundary which separates 'us' from 'them', and the distinction would probably be recognized on both sides of that boundary. Ethnicity is a multifaceted phenomenon based on physical appearance, subjective identification [how a group sees itself], cultural and religious affiliation, stereotyping and social exclusion.
>
> (Modood and Berthoud 1997, p. 13)

Research and evaluation activity

List the essential features of an ethnic group described in the above quotation. Identify which ethnic groups are represented in your A-level sociology group.

Measuring ethnic diversity in Britain

The official government method of measuring the extent of ethnic diversity is through the Census, which is carried out on a national basis every ten years. The 1991 Census asked this question about people's ethnicity:

Ethnic group *(please tick the appropriate box)*

☐ White
☐ Black Caribbean
☐ Black African
☐ Black other (please specify)
☐ Indian
☐ Pakistani
☐ Bangladeshi
☐ Chinese
☐ Any other ethnic group (please describe)

If the person is descended from more than one ethnic or racial group, please tick the group to which the person considers he/she belongs, or tick the 'Any other ethnic group' box and describe the person's ancestry in the space provided.

The Census data provided the following picture of ethnic diversity in Britain:

Table 8.1 Ethnic diversity in Britain

Ethnic group	% of the population
White	94.51
All ethnic minorities	5.49
'All ethnic minorities' comprises:	
Black Caribbean	0.91
Black African	0.39
Black other	0.33
Indian	1.53
Pakistani	0.87
Bangladeshi	0.30
Chinese	0.29
Other – Asian	0.36
Other – other	0.53

Source: Peach (1996), p. 8

We can distinguish between *ethnic groups* and *ethnic minority groups*. In the above statistics, the 5.49 per cent figure for 'all ethnic minorities' is made up of a variety of ethnic minority groups. 'Minority' refers to (1) groups that are *numerically* in a minority and (2) groups that are *economically*, *politically* and *culturally* in a minority owing to various forms of discrimination.

There are some things about this Census data which are not altogether helpful to sociologists. Many of the groups identified in the Census data really comprise several different ethnic subgroups. The quotation from Modood and Berthoud (p. 113) reminds us, for example, that the white group contains several ethnicities defined with reference to *culture*: Irish, Welsh, Scots, Polish, Australian, etc. These groups may have different religious affiliations and different levels of religiosity. We will see the significance of this in a discussion of religion in Northern Ireland later in this chapter (see pp. 126–8).

This possibility of subdividing the white group also applies to all the other groups identified in the Census. The black Caribbean group is not homogeneous in terms of culture: people from Jamaica, for example, have elements of culture – cooking, for instance – quite distinct from those of people from Trinidad. Equally, there are cultural differences within the Chinese population.

There is no reference in the Census data to the things that people often see as essential to their ethnicity and to their culture. The idea of being British or English, for example, seems to be an important part of many people's **ethnic and cultural identity**, but the category 'British' or 'English' would include people from many different groups in the Census data – white British, Caribbean British, black British, Indian British – and people with different religious affiliations.

Although we must always bear in mind these difficulties concerning the Census data on ethnicity, we will see that the ethnic groups that are identified do allow us to say some significant things about relationships between ethnicity and religion.

Religion and ethnic diversity

The ethnic data from the Census can be linked to broad patterns of religious affiliation.

Table 8.2 Ethnicity and religious affiliation

Ethnic group	Main religious affiliation
White	Christian
Black Caribbean	Christian
Black African	Christian; Muslim
Indian	Hindu; Muslim; Sikh
Pakistani	Muslim
Bangladeshi	Muslim; Hindu
Chinese	Buddhist; Confucian; Taoist

The data from the 1991 Census demonstrate that Britain is ethnically diverse: there is a wide range of ethnic groups with different religious affiliations, and there are more ethnic groups than are identified in the Census data. We can now look at the role religion plays in how people think of themselves as ethnic groups; this forms part of Modood and Berthoud's (1997) analysis of the 1991 Census data on ethnicity.

We can combine two aspects of Modood and Berthoud's views to say that ethnicity comprises:

● *subjective identification*: with which ethnicity do I and my group identify?

● *religious identification*: to what extent does it help construct ethnicity?

A number of general points can be made about religious affiliation among ethnic minority groups; that is, those people comprising the 5.49 per cent of the population identified in the Census as non-white. First, however we choose to measure religious affiliation, most ethnic minority groups are more religious than the majority population. Table 8.3 shows the results of a survey conducted in Britain which asked respondents to state their religious affiliation: the table lists the responses of people from the majority white population (first column) and people from ethnic minority groups (the remaining columns). Responses are given as percentages.

Table 8.3 Measuring religious affiliation

	White (exc. Irish)	Irish	Caribbean	Indian	African Asian	Pakistani	Bangladeshi	Chinese
None	31	14	28	5	2	2	1	58
Hindu	–	–	1	32	58	–	2	–
Sikh	–	–	–	50	19	–	–	–
Muslim	–	–	1	6	15	96	95	–
Christian	68	85	69	5	3	–	1	23
Other	1	1	3	2	3	2	1	19
Weighted count	2755	110	1567	1292	799	862	285	391
Unweighted count	2746	119	1205	1273	728	1185	591	214

Source: Modood and Berthoud (1997), table 9.5, p. 298

Interpretation activity

What do the figures in Table 8.3 tell us about levels of religiosity among the majority white population and among ethnic minority groups? Which groups have the highest and the lowest levels of religiosity?

Second, Modood and Berthoud (1997, p. 298) show that there are gender differences in religious affiliation among some ethnic minority groups. For example, 75 per cent of Afro-Caribbean women said they were religious, compared with less than 66 per cent of the men. Third, there are also age-related differences, with religiosity declining with age in some sectors of ethnic minority groups.

Grace Davie suggests some general reasons why religion seems to be more important for ethnic minority groups than for the majority population:

Minorities almost always behave differently from majorities with respect to both [religious] belief and belonging. For there are, undoubtedly, certain pressures on a community which derive from its minority status; a status which poses inevitable questions about identity, about the maintenance of a tradition, about the future of the group in question. Not surprisingly, religious practice tends to be high in such communities, who may feel a certain responsibility to encourage a continuity that is unsupported in the mainstream.

(Davie 1994, p. 111)

Minorities can therefore be expected to exhibit relatively high levels of religiosity for the following reasons:

- Many ethnic minority groups originate from societies with high levels of religiosity; for example, the Asian subcontinent.

- Maintaining a commitment to religion can act as a basis for community solidarity in a new environment.

- There is often strong family pressure to maintain religious commitment.

- Maintaining a religious commitment is also a way to maintain other aspects of cultural identity, such as language, art, patterns of marriage, cooking and so on.

Islam, Hinduism and Sikhism among ethnic minorities of South Asian origin

Research activity

List the variety of ethnic minority groups in your locality by identifying each group's places of worship.

Defining terms

- 'Islam' is the general name of a particular religion.
- A 'Muslim' is someone who accepts Islam.
- The Census data suggest that Asian populations in Britain are of South Asian origin, that is, from the Indian subcontinent. This is rather a simplistic view and ignores the real history of Asian migrations. There are populations of South Asian origin in many of the islands of the Caribbean. More importantly, there were significant populations of Asian people in some of the countries of East Africa, for example Uganda. Much of this population, which was predominantly either Hindu or Sikh, migrated to Britain in the 1960s in response to economic and political harassment. For this reason, the term 'Asian' should not simply be equated, for example, with 'Indian' or 'Pakistani'. As with many such groups that have been dispersed through migration, they live in many different places while maintaining some Asian identity.

We saw in Table 8.3 that people of South Asian origin have high levels of religiosity compared with the majority white population; only a very small proportion of people of Indian origin, for example, say they have no religious affiliation (see p. 115).

Why are there high levels of religious commitment among people of South Asian origin? To what extent does such religious commitment have a social function, as Bruce (1995) suggests? There are two ways of answering these questions: one broadly describes the social function of religious affiliation, while the other refers to

how religious affiliation concerns relationships between the minority and the majority populations.

Social functions of religious commitment

We can indicate the social functions of religious commitment by referring to processes of migration. South Asian migration to Britain occurred, for example, in the 1950s and 1960s and involved single people and married people without their families.

Migration: patterns and reasons

Britain has experienced immigration – people *entering* the country – and emigration – people *leaving* the country – for a very long time. For example, French Protestant Huguenots moved to England in the seventeenth century; there was significant Irish immigration in the nineteenth century; and in the twentieth century many people emigrated to Australia and New Zealand. It is these *patterns* of migration that have made Britain a culturally and religiously diverse society.

There are distinct *reasons* why people have moved to Britain. For example, immigration from the New Commonwealth (the Caribbean and the Asian subcontinent) in the 1950s and 1960s occurred for two sets of reasons. There were factors pulling people into Britain, among them a high demand for labour in certain parts of the economy (hospitals, for example) and consequent active recruitment by the British government on behalf of British companies. There were also factors pushing people out of the Caribbean and the Asian subcontinent. These included rural impoverishment, which was partly a consequence of colonization.

Many migrants from South Asia were Hindu, Muslim or Sikh, but they arrived in a society with a predominantly Christian religious heritage. There were therefore few opportunities for migrants to practise their religion. The opportunities increased with the arrival of more people of similar religious affiliation and as temples, mosques and other places of worship were constructed. Once religious organizations were established, religious affiliation became a basis of support for new migrants: a point of contact in a new country, a source of marriage partners, social welfare and so on. In this sense, religion was *socially functional* – it aided adjustment to a new society and encouraged the maintenance of cultural identity.

Religious affiliation and relationships between minority and majority populations

However, religion also played a crucial role in mediating relationships between the migrant and other populations. In the case of South Asian migration, there is a number of significant issues that should be noted.

- The wider society was either predominantly Christian or of no religion; it was certainly an increasingly *secularized* society. (See Chapters 6 and 7 for more on secularization.) Migrant populations maintained their distinctiveness through a commitment to religion, which also helped them to articulate their views about the wider society.

- The British system of education gave insufficient attention to religion and was *de facto* Christian: forms of worship in schools were Christian. This led to criticisms from Muslim parents, for example.

The importance of Hindu religious tradition. Neasden temple, north London.

Education and religion

The 1944 Education Act only permitted the teaching of *Christian* religion in schools and specified Christian worship. It also established voluntary-aided schools: Christian church schools funded by the state. The 1988 Education Reform Act still did not allow state funding for schools of non-Christian religions, but it changed the rules on religious worship and the teaching of religion:

> [The syllabus in religion] should reflect the fact that the religious traditions of Great Britain are in the main Christian whilst taking account of the teachings and practices of the other principal religions represented in Great Britain.
>
> (1988 Education Reform Act: 8.3)

In effect, the 1988 Act includes some religious traditions – Islam and Judaism, for example – but excludes others – Rastafarianism, for example. The Act also established multi-faith worship in schools so that religious worship could reflect a range of religious traditions.

When the 1988 Education Reform Act allowed multi-faith worship, many ethnic minority groups regarded this in itself as problematic: multi-faith worship was thought to dilute traditional religious ideas. Another sign of the prioritization of Christian religion was the existence of state-funded religious schools for Christians, which contrasts, for example, with the absence of publicly-funded Muslim schools.

School decision triumph for blacks

The Seventh Day Adventists yesterday became the first minor Christian denomination to win state funding for a school when the Government said it was satisfied with standards at John Loughborough secondary in Haringey, north London.

Stephen Byers, the education standards minister, told the school it would get a full public grant from September and be allowed to increase its intake from 139 to 250 pupils. It will be given temporary grant-maintained status, but will probably become an aided school later this year with the same rights as Anglican, Methodist and Catholic establishments.

The school was set up 18 years ago in response to the dissatisfaction of many black Christian teachers and parents with mainstream state education. These concerns grew over recent years because of evidence that expulsions of black children from mainstream schools were disproportionately high.

Source: *The Guardian*, 10 March 1998

State funding of schools representing smaller Christian denominations, such as the Seventh Day Adventist Church, occurred just ahead of state funding for Muslim schools, which happened in the summer of 1998.

Britain's first Islamic school looks like getting state funding

Yusuf Islam, formerly the singer Cat Stevens, was cautiously hopeful as he strode through a melee of small boys pursuing a tennis ball around the playground of Islamia School, the school he founded. His frustrating battle to get it admitted to the state education sector is now closer than at any time in more than a decade.

The 1993 Education Act, which allowed independent schools to apply to become grant-maintained, allows ministers and their advisers to take choice and diversity into account as well as value for money and surplus places. In Islamia's case, an 800-long waiting list for a school of 180 pupils who come from all over London proved 'a very powerful piece of evidence', according to one Funding Agency for Schools source.

Source: *The Guardian,* 21 January 1997

Muslims stand their ground

Wendy Berliner hears some strong arguments from Muslim schools for a fairer share of funding and visits one seeking voluntary-aided status.

'PART of the British establishment hoodwinks itself into thinking this is a white, Anglo-Saxon, Christian country,' says Moeen Yaseen, a spokesman for the Muslim Education Forum. 'It will be a long-term battle to remove the inequalities.'

There are 250,000 Muslim schoolchildren in this country, the largest concentration of non-Anglican children after Roman Catholics. Most of them go to state schools. There are 28 private Muslim schools educating about 2,500 children. Most but not all of these want to join the state sector. About six of the schools for older children offer religious training for pupils preparing for a vocation. Two are schools for children of expatriate workers, well resourced and separate.

The Education Reform Act of 1988 says that RE syllabuses must 'reflect the fact that religious traditions in Great Britain are, in the main, Christian while taking account of the teaching of other principal religions that are represented in Great Britain.'

… Religious education is outside the national curriculum but remains compulsory even in the sixth form. In theory, non-Christian parents can withdraw their children from religious-education lessons and ask for alternative religious classes. In practice, says Dr Pasha, non-Christian parents are subtly persuaded not to. 'Our parents are told by headteachers that there will be no-one to supervise their children is they withdraw them. Sometimes our parents are not aware of their rights, sometimes there are language problems.'

… 'A Muslim school offers positive models of practising Muslim professionals, male and female,' Moeen Yaseen says. 'It represents Muslim values as well as freedom of religion, uniform, prayers, food, diet and holidays, Arabic and Islamic studies. In a Muslim school you don't have to fight for these basic rights. The government of the school is in Muslim hands.'

TWIXT CHURCH AND STATE

Voluntary-aided schools were established by the 1944 Education Act as a compromise between Church and State. Under the Act, public funds can augment the resources of the churches which would otherwise have been unable to develop their all-age schools into separate primary and secondary schools, as the Act required.

More school places were needed because of war damage to schools and a rising post-war birth rate. Voluntary schools receive 85 per cent of building costs from the Government and all running costs from the local authority.

There are nearly 4,000 voluntary-aided schools. Church of England schools are just in the majority with 1,875. There are 1,817 Roman Catholic schools, 17 Jewish and 4 Methodist.

Source: *The Guardian,* 23 March 1998

For South Asian populations, especially those who are Muslim, there is a particular problem connected with education for girls. Islam has certain views on relationships between men and women and boys and girls. These include ideas about how some aspects of education should be segregated (for example, sex education) and appropriate dress codes, which affect participation in sports. These views are difficult to accommodate in the existing education system, which is predominantly co-educational with few single-sex schools. There are similar issues about clothing requirements (for example, the Sikh requirement for boys to wear a form of turban) and about diet (Islam, Hinduism and Sikhism all have rules about food which have often not been considered within the school system).

Many schools try to accommodate religious needs and uniform codes.

Religion, therefore, becomes a way of maintaining a minority cultural identity – maintaining Islamic dress codes and Asian languages, for example – within a mainly white, Christian society. Religion is socially functional and becomes a basis for resisting processes of assimilation.

Christmas comes but once a year – to all

Hindu

Materialism may gull but carols can chime well with India's pantheistic faith

'Theologically, Christmas is not a problem for us. Hindus believe whenever there is an increase of evil in the world, God becomes incarnate. We see Christ as another incarnation of God to show us the right path. I try to inculcate in my children a sense of the family of religions and that they are not all at odds with each other.'

At Christmas, the Kadodwala boys go carol singing for charity, and at school they learn about the nativity. At home they celebrate with relatives over a special biryani.

Muslim

A delicate balancing act in preserving Islamic tradition and building bridges

'There is a delicate balancing act to be done,' says Mr Darr, who feels both the worry of preserving Islamic traditions and beliefs in a non-Islamic country, and the need to build bridges to Bradford's other communities and faiths.

His shop is noted for such bridge building – it stocks the region's largest collection of Afro-Caribbean books, and opened this summer with a calypso flourish by John Agard, the Guyanese humorous poet. But many Muslim customers don't want things to change too far, too fast.

Jewish

'These days the kosher bakeries are full of mince pies'

Sharon has begun to enjoy the festivities. 'I had never had Christmas pudding until after I got married. These days the kosher bakeries are full of mince pies – it adds richness to the season. The neighbours had a Christmas tree and we went round with the children to see it, then we had Suker tabernacle for Sukot and they came and enjoyed the decorations.'

Source: *The Guardian*, 23 December 1996

The dominant political framework established for dealing with ethnic diversity emphasizes **assimilation**: minorities should, as far as possible, take on the culture of the majority and therefore give up their own cultures. This is particularly the case in the public sphere of work, education and so on: little recognition may be accorded to ethnic minority languages and cultures in formal schooling, for example, but it is perfectly acceptable in the private sphere of the home.

Interpretation activity

How far do the Hindu, Muslim and Jewish responses to Christmas in the newspaper article on the previous page suggest a process of assimilation?

I say Amen, you say Om

When Dad's a devout Christian and Mum's a Hindu, what's to become of the children?

A rabbi at Maidstone synagogue, Dr Romain has counselled more than 2,000 mixed-faith couples and identifies parenting as the greatest pressure point in the relationship, even for those couples who lack deep religious convictions. 'Very often couples who got on well when it was just the two of them hit problems when children arrive,' he explains. 'A lot of people underestimate their own religious feelings, regarding themselves as lapsed or agnostic. But when it comes to children, their religion brings an enormously emotive tug. People are surprised at how they feel about issues they had dismissed for 30 years.'

Usually, the partner with the stronger belief holds sway, just as Cherie Blair, a committed Catholic, did over the question of raising her children. When Denise Williams, a practising Jew, wanted her children – Mark and Joanna – brought up in her faith, she was helped by the willingness of her husband Hugh, a Christian. 'At first we thought about not putting them into any religion at all,' says Denise, 'but I felt very strongly that Judaism was my children's birthright. Fortunately, Hugh has always supported me.'

When both partners have a strong faith, the likelihood of conflict is much greater – a problem faced by the Reverend Derek Barnes and his wife, Rohini, a devout Hindu. Despite Derek's position at the heart of the Anglican church, the couple have educated their sons in both religions, baptising them as babies but also taking them to the local temple and filling their vicarage at Holy Trinity Church, Southall, with paintings of Hindu divinities. Recently, however, the eldest, Himal, now 14, stopped attending church, opting to follow his mother's faith exclusively.

The pressures are hardly eased by the religions themselves. With 72 per cent of Catholics and 44 per cent of Jews now 'marrying out', along with growing numbers of Muslims, Sikhs and Hindus, religious leaders are concerned about further dilution of faith. While many now profess greater tolerance of mixed-faith marriages, it doesn't yet extend to the fruit of such unions. The Roman Catholic Church in Scotland recently published a report encouraging debate, but it still insists that the Catholic partner do everything to ensure children are brought up in the faith.

Source: *The Guardian*, 9 December 1998

From the article about mixed-faith marriages, what difficulties do you think that the children of such unions face in the process of assimilation?

It is important to recognize that resisting assimilation is rarely entirely successful. Even though religiosity among people of South Asian origin has been maintained (see Table 8.3 on p. 115, above), there is still a tendency for it to decline among the young:

> In a country such as Britain where religious pluralism is still not formally recognized, many British Asians, be they Muslim, Sikh or Hindu, have chosen, conditionally at least, to preserve and uphold the religious and cultural doctrines of their parents. The holding on to such doctrines can provide a kind of 'empowerment through difference', but many second-generation Asians also carefully negotiate their associations with religion. Issues such as choice of marriage partners, intra-ethnic marriage and diet … often lead to the adoption of a position of selective cultural preference; a kind of code switching in which young Asians move between one culture and another, depending on context and whether overt 'Britishness' or pronounced 'Asianness' is most appropriate.
>
> (Johal 1998, p. 7)

Interpretation activity

Why are young Asians 'code switching'? To what extent is it part of the process of secularization discussed in Chapters 6 and 7?

Religion and the Afro-Caribbean population

The migration of Afro-Caribbean peoples was most significant in the 1950s and 1960s and occurred for the reasons mentioned on pp. 117–18, above. A distinctive feature of this migration was that migrants had relatively high levels of religiosity compared with the indigenous population, and that the religious tradition of Afro-Caribbean people was predominantly Christian. Within that tradition, Afro-Caribbean people were more likely to be Pentecostal than Anglican.

Pentecostalism

> The Pentecostalist movement, by far the largest group of African-Caribbean Christians, is directly related to the Azusa Street Revival under the leadership of William J. Seymour in Los Angeles from 1906. This reasserted African elements in … Christianity, of which two characteristics are 'speaking in tongues', believed to include actual languages given to improve communication between God and people, and divine healing, understood as redemption of the individual and the community. … The largest multi-congregational Pentecostal body in the United States is the Assembly of God, with an inclusive membership of about 2.1 million in 1988 … [there are] three different families of the black Pentecostal movement in Britain … the largest number of adherents is [to] the Trinitarian Pentecostals. … Their teaching is represented by two sister organizations, the New Testament Church of God … and the Church of God of Prophecy. … The second family of Pentecostals in Britain is the Oneness (Apostolic) Pentecostals. … This organization … was popular … among the black and urban poor in Jamaica. … In the United Kingdom, approximately one third of all Pentecostals are members of this

movement. The movement's outreach work, ecumenical relations and community projects mean that it is still attracting adherents. ... The third black Pentecostal family is the Revival (Healing) Pentecostals ... [its] healing campaigns unite black and white interracially.

(Hennels 1997, pp. 722–3)

Afro-Caribbean migrants found religion in Britain to be very different from the religion they experienced in the Caribbean. The typical British Anglican church service was dominated by older people and women, and required little participation from the congregation. Conversely, the typical Pentecostal church encouraged extensive participation by all age groups, was not dominated by women, and required considerable involvement from worshippers, including dancing and call-and-response between congregation and clergy. Pentecostalism also places greater emphasis on religious experience than on religious dogma and teaching, stresses the importance of conversion experiences and their public acknowledgement, and believes in the power of religion to heal people, both physically and mentally.

Pentecostalism has played a dual role for Afro-Caribbean people. For some, it has become a way to adjust to a society in which Afro-Caribbean people face discrimination and racial injustice; in that sense, it is close to the form of 'social opium' which Marx described, and illustrates Weber's idea that some religious groups successfully recruit and meet the needs of the underprivileged (see Chapter 2, pp. 18–19 and Chapter 4, pp. 50–4). However, Pentecostalism can also help to improve a person's socio-economic status. As Pryce (1979) suggests, Pentecostalism encouraged hard work, strict sexual morality, careful and diligent acquisition of wealth, and the support of family and religious community. In that sense, it has some of the features of the Protestant ethic which Weber saw as essential to the development of capitalism (see Chapter 10, pp. 150–4).

Rastafarianism as a religion of the oppressed

In part because of its association with the music of Bob Marley, Rastafarianism has received considerable popular attention. A religious movement rooted in the Old Testament of the Christian Bible, it developed in Jamaica in the 1920s. Among other things, it preached that black people needed to return to Africa if they were to be saved, in particular, from economic deprivation and racial discrimination. It regarded Jamaica as a place of evil, equivalent to the biblical Babylon. In these ways, Rastafarianism is a typical religious sect based on material underprivilege; as such, it fits in with Weber's analysis of sect development (see Chapter 4, pp. 50–4). The visit to Jamaica of the Emperor of Ethiopia, Haile Selassie, in the 1950s, was interpreted by Rastafarians as the sign of their imminent return to Africa, and Selassie became the prophet of the movement.

Rastafarianism has become important in Britain, particularly for Afro-Caribbean men. We can describe three varieties of Rastafarianism: one which remains faithful to the original religious message of redemption through return to Africa; one which takes a more political form and, for example, sponsors people to stand for elections in Jamaica; and one which is predominantly cultural, in which adherents sport the symbols of Rastafarianism – hair, style of dress, diet – without a detailed knowledge of its theology. The second and third forms of Rastafarianism have generally abandoned the idea of a real return to Africa; instead, they favour the transformation of Rastafarians' present homelands into Zion (a biblical name for a place of justice and peace).

Summary

In summary, we can say that religion plays a crucial role for ethnic minority groups as they adjust to a new society, defend their cultural identities and strive to improve their socio-economic status. For example, the expansion of Asian businesses, particularly in food retailing, is related both to the demand among Muslims for particular kinds of food unavailable in the mainstream, and also a wider demand for a variety of foods from the majority white population. This expansion has enhanced the economic success and socio-economic status of people in the population of Asian origin.

As Bruce (1996) argues, religious tradition is therefore both essential and unrecoverable once it is lost:

> Once a religious culture has become fragmented, and the close ties between religion and ethnicity lost, then no amount of external pressure will recreate a shared religious tradition and restore it to a central place in cultural defence.
>
> (Bruce 1996, p. 123)

A Jewish community in London

Robert Ash and Ian Goodchild's (1997) study of a Jewish community in London highlights some interesting issues about how religious communities adapt to new social situations. Bruce (1996) argues that religion is, for ethnic minorities, a form of social defence, which allows traditions to be maintained in the face of new social situations. According to Ash and Goodchild (1997), it is not quite as simple as that. They studied the formation of an *eruv* in London by a group of Jewish people. An *eruv* is an area (a street, a group of streets, or an entire community) in which Jewish people can carry objects on the Sabbath. Such an area is necessary because the Jewish faith prohibits people from carrying almost anything on the Sabbath, even things that are crucial for day-to-day life. The particular *eruv* Ash and Goodchild discuss would cover most of the London Borough of Barnet, traditionally an area with a high Jewish population. What is especially interesting about the opposition to the planning application for the *eruv* is that much of it came from ultra-Orthodox Jews, while most of its support came from prosperous, middle-class professional people. Ash and Goodchild comment:

> We suggest that the desire, on the part of a highly integrated Anglo-Jewish population, to establish what some perceive as an anachronistic, almost totemic, religious symbol in a modern London suburb, represents rather the assertion of a new type of Jewish Orthodox identity ... in late modern societies ... assimilation to unitary common cultures is no longer possible; there are no unitary cultures in late modernity.
>
> (Ash and Goodchild 1997, pp. 12–13)

Ash and Goodchild believe that such people are creating new religious identities for themselves, and that this constitutes more than just cultural defence: it suggests that religious cultures can be maintained and revitalized. We will return to a discussion of late modernity in Chapter 11.

Religion in Northern Ireland

The significance of religion in Northern Ireland is demonstrated in one of its most important annual parades:

> The Twelfth of July parade is an act of commemoration, a time to perpetuate and celebrate the memory of a three-hundred-year-old battle when the Catholic King James was defeated by the Protestant King William and the Protestant ascendancy was established. ... Each year the events of July 1690

are replayed, the march to battle and back now condensed into a single day … [Protestant] unity is created in opposition to those who are excluded from the day's events, the Roman Catholic population, who are allowed no part in the proceedings, and are in some cases virtually imprisoned for the day, as daily routine is put on hold. … The day is an occasion when the city of Belfast … becomes a totally Protestant city.

(Jarman 1997, pp. 106–8)

British colonialism in Ireland

Protestant parades establish a link between the present, in which Protestants see themselves as politically dominant in Northern Ireland, and the long history of British colonialism. The whole of what is now Eire and Northern Ireland was colonized by the British, who were also Protestant, in the seventeenth century. The major part of this process was the settlement of British landowners, who took control of land from the indigenous Irish population. In Protestant parades, a political victory is also commemorated as a religious victory and the whole history of British settlement is remembered through the lens of a particular religious tradition.

Jarman notes that the Roman Catholic communities of Northern Ireland also hold parades, but far fewer than on the Protestant side: in 1995, there were some 2,580 Protestant parades compared with 300 on what is often called the Republican side (Jarman 1997, p. 119). What do these parades tell us about the role of religion in Northern Ireland?

Religion and identity

Richard Jenkins (1997) suggests that the identity of different social groups in Northern Ireland is complex and religion is just one of several indicators of such identity. Each religious group also has other ways in which it is defined and in terms of which it thinks about its identity (see Table 8.4).

Table 8.4 Religion and identity in Northern Ireland

Protestant	Roman Catholic
British	Irish
Ulster(men)	Feinians
Unionist	Republican
Loyalist	Republican
Orangemen	Nationalist

Religious identification is therefore important, but other aspects of identity become important depending on circumstances. Protestants often define themselves as loyalist when they assert that Northern Ireland should remain part of the United Kingdom; many Roman Catholics do not define themselves as nationalists, but are likely to identify themselves as Republicans when the same issue of a united Ireland becomes significant.

Religious affiliation in Northern Ireland is extremely important in understanding the behaviour of social groups. According to most measures of religiosity, the people of Northern Ireland – Protestant and Roman Catholic – are more religious than people on the UK mainland; they are more likely to attend church, to do so regularly, and to define themselves as members of religious organizations (see Bruce 1986). Not only are they more religious, but there is also a complex relationship between religion, where people live and their political beliefs. Many parts of Northern Ireland are territorially segregated: this is the case in Belfast, for example, where very high proportions of people live in areas where the overwhelming majority are of the same religion (Boal 1982). The significance of this territorial arrangement is indicated in the views of British people generally. Table 8.5 summarizes interviewees' responses to a questionnaire which asked them how close they felt to the different groups of people listed in the left-hand column:

Table 8.5 People feel closer to some groups than to others.

	Very close %	Fairly close %	A little close %	Not very close %	Not at all close %
For you personally, how close would you say you feel towards people who:					
were born in the same area as you?	9.8	39.5	26.3	14.0	8.8
have the same social background as yours?	10.2	48.6	27.4	9.1	3.1
have the same religious background as yours?	8.8	26.8	26.2	20.4	15.0
are of the same race as you?	13.8	42.2	25.9	10.5	5.4
live in the same area as you do now?	8.9	37.2	32.2	14.8	5.3
have the same political beliefs as you?	7.0	27.1	30.8	20.9	11.5

Source: Brook (1992), p. 3

Interpretation activity

What do these figures tell us about the importance of religious background and other forms of identification in defining social and community solidarity in Northern Ireland?

The point about these figures is that they all reflect the territorial segregation of major populations of Northern Ireland. The idea that sharing the same religion, the same social background, and so on, is significant, is itself a product of where people live, with whom they socialize, and whom they marry.

How, then, do we measure and assess the significance of religion in Northern Ireland?

Assessing the significance of religion in Northern Ireland

- Religion is believed by many in Northern Ireland to structure their lives. For example, there is opposition to mixed marriages in both Protestant and Roman Catholic communities.

- Education is generally segregated along religious lines.

- Patterns of unemployment are related to religious affiliation: unemployment among Catholics is highest.

- Some Unionist politicians are also religious people and simultaneously hold political and religious office – Reverend Ian Paisley is both a religious official and leader of the Ulster Democratic Unionist Party.

- Religious affiliations influence political views. For example, Protestants tend to be concerned about the prominent role of the Roman Catholic Church in the Irish Republic and see this as a major reason for opposing a united Ireland. That the actual role of the Roman Catholic Church is quite different to many Protestants' beliefs about it – and that not all Roman Catholics want a united Ireland – is often ignored.

Although religion structures a great deal of social life in Northern Ireland, there are issues about which different religions share the same views – opposition to abortion, for example. Religion provides a significant basis for how social life is organized, but it is not the cause of the divisions which exist. A sociological understanding of Northern Ireland suggests that the fundamental issues are relationships with the United Kingdom, nationalism and ethnic domination. Religion structures these concerns and becomes a rationale for dealing with them: both Protestants and Roman Catholics fear that the other's religion will help subjugate them.

Conclusion

The study of religions in an ethnically diverse society challenges some of the central ideas of the sociology of religion – for example, how sociologists have classified religious organization. Religions in an ethnically diverse society are also important for minorities in maintaining cultural identity and resisting majority cultures; the same religions may also enhance, inhibit or change minority groups.

Essay question

Discuss, with examples, the extent to which religion assists ethnic minorities to integrate in new social situations. To what extent do ethnic minority religious traditions remain unchanged in this process?

References and further reading

Ash, R. and Goodchild, I. (1997) 'Poles apart – secularisation and Anglo-Jewry', *Sociology Review*, 7:1, pp. 9–13.

Boal, F. (1982) 'Segregating and mixing: space and residence in Belfast', in F. Boal and J. Douglas (eds), *Integration and Division*, London: Academic Press, pp. 249–80.

Brook, L. (1992) *British Social Attitudes: Cumulative Source Book, the first six surveys*, London: Gower.

Bruce, S. (1986) *God save Ulster: The religion and politics of Paisleyism*, Oxford: Oxford University Press.

Bruce, S. (1995) *Religion in Modern Britain*, Oxford: Oxford University Press.

Bruce, S. (1996) *Religion in the Modern World: From cathedrals to cults*, Oxford: Oxford University Press.

Davie, G. (1994) *Religion in Britain since 1945: Believing without belonging*, Oxford: Blackwell.

Hinnells, J. (1997) *The New Handbook of Living Religions*, London: Blackwell.

Jarman, N. (1997) *Material Conflicts: Parades and visual display in Northern Ireland*, Oxford: Berg.

Jenkins, R. (1997) *Rethinking Ethnicity*, London: Sage.

Johal, S. (1998) 'Brimful of Brasia', *Sociology Review*, 8:1, pp. 5–8.

Modood, T. and Berthoud, R. *et al* (1997) *Ethnic Minorities in Britain: Diversity and disadvantage*, The Fourth National Survey of Ethnic Minorites, London: Policy Studies Institute.

Peach, C. (1996) 'Ethnicity in the 1991 Census', *The Ethnic Minority Populations of Great Britain*, Vol. 2, London: HMSO.

Pryce, K. (1979) *Endless Pressure: A study of West Indian lifestyles in Bristol*, Harmondsworth: Penguin.

9 Gender and religion

Key terms	Key thinkers
Gender	Grace Davie
Social divisions	Jane Holm
Patriarchy	John Bowker
Secularization	Steve Bruce
New religious movements	Max Weber
New age movements	Elizabeth Puttick
Fundamentalism	John Hawley
Ordination	Helen Watson
	Charlotte Butler
	Mohammed Anwar
	Sylvia Walby

Introduction

In Chapter 3 (pp. 38–40) we noted that women are more likely than men to have religious beliefs and to practise their religion. This chapter will examine such **gender** differences in more detail and attempt to explain them. It will discuss the relationship between **patriarchy** and religion, and study the role of women in **new religious movements**, **new age movements** and in various forms of religious **fundamentalism**. Two case studies are included: one on the debate about the **ordination** of women to the priesthood in the Church of England, another on women in Islam in Britain.

Throughout, it will be important to bear in mind that – despite many sociological studies on gender and gender identity – relatively little has been written about *religion and gender*.

> ### Research activity
>
> Look at the A-level sociology textbooks in your school or college library. Do they have sections on religion and gender? What percentage of the whole text do they devote to the subject? Make a list of the topics covered.

Gender, social divisions and patriarchy

Sociologists interest themselves in those kinds of social divisions that affect people's *life chances* (such things as income, skills, property) and *lifestyles* (such things as patterns of consumption, and attitudes and values). The major social divisions include class, gender, ethnicity and age; all of these tend to produce inequality. This inequality can be gauged by measuring, for example, people's comparative wealth, income, status and political power. We note how religion relates to issues of social class in Chapter 10, ethnicity in Chapter 8 and age and gender in Chapter 9. This chapter will examine in more detail the relationships between gender and religion.

Those social divisions connected with gender are distinct from others: they are social *status* divisions that give rise to a structure of inequality which sociologists call **patriarchy**. Whereas, for example, social *class* divisions are associated with wealth, property, income and related life *chances* – such things as access to good healthcare and expensive holidays – *gender* is best seen as a *status* division, which is associated with life *styles* – such things as values, ways of life, and the assumptions about these things made by other gender groups. A person's social class position *and* status position affect his or her access to power.

This suggests that there is a complex relationship between gender divisions and social class divisions. For example, women's exclusion from employment opportunities at the highest level – what has been called the 'glass ceiling' – is often explained by reference to assumptions about their status as women. Assumptions about gender can become the basis for disadvantaging women and excluding them from, for example, the upper hierarchy of many religious organizations.

The structure of inequality based on gender divisions is generally labelled **patriarchy**. Patriarchy can be defined as male domination of women. It operates across a whole range of institutional settings: the household, the economy, the culture, in education and in terms of sexuality. Patriarchy is both *individual* (for example, those individual men who abuse their wives or partners) and *structural* (for example, the under-representation of women in the judiciary). Many feminist theorists (for example, Walby 1992) claim that patriarchy has a very long history and that it remains strong, despite major changes in the status of women. As we will see, religion plays a part in the maintenance of patriarchy.

Gender, religious practice and religious belief

There are major gender differences in religious practice and religious belief: such things as attendance at religious services, ideas about God and the importance placed on private prayer.

The statistics presented in Chapter 3 (p. 38) suggest that, at least as far as the

Christian churches are concerned, women are more likely to attend worship and to do so regularly: 66 per cent of regular churchgoers are women. Walker (1990) asserts that women are also more likely to engage in private prayer, while Davie (1994) suggests that women also have distinct patterns of religious belief: she cites evidence from Jacobs and Worcester's 1994 study.

Davie also shows that men and women view God in distinct ways, which are themselves gendered; women see God as a god of love, comfort and forgiveness, while men are more likely to see God as a god of power and control. These different views of God are said to be *gendered* because:

● they divide along gender lines: men tend to have one view and women another;

Belief in (%):					
	God	Sin	Evil	Devil	Life after death
Women	84	72	76	42	57
Men	75	66	58	32	39

Source: Davie (1994)

● the attributes ascribed to God have been traditionally regarded as characteristic either of men or women.

Davie supports Walker's (1990) assertion that women are much more likely than men to regard private prayer as important and much more likely to actually practise it.

Walker and Davie are agreed that women are more religious than men and also have different religious beliefs – beliefs connected with existing assumptions about gender itself. Why are there these differences between men and women? There are many possible responses to this question.

First, we could draw on the work of Weber (1922b/1978) and argue that women are more religious precisely because – in a patriarchal society – they are less powerful than men: religiosity acts as a form of compensation for underprivilege. Weber was convinced that this function of religion was a major reason why women were so prominent in many religious sects. Bruce (1996, pp. 219–20) points to women's key role in establishing the Seventh Day Adventist Church (Ellen White), Christian Science (Mary Baker Eddy) and the Shaker movement (Ann Lee).

Mary Baker Eddy (pictured in 1886) established the first Church of Christ, Scientist in 1879. In 1995, she was inducted into the US National Women's Hall of Fame.

Second, some feminist theorists (for example, Holm 1994) argue that religion does not so much *compensate* for women's disadvantaged social position as *reflect* it. The subordinate role of women in society generally is reflected in their subordinate role within many religious organizations; a subordinate role that is maintained by men's domination of those same organizations. Arguably, the maleness of many gods and the predominance of men in many religious hierarchies indicate this pattern of subordination and domination.

Third, Bruce (1996, pp. 220–1) links the greater religiosity of women to the process of **secularization** discussed in Chapters 6 and 7. He argues that, as this process has occurred, religion has become much more of a personal matter expressed in the private sphere of the home. As women generally continue to be far more active in the home than men, they are also likely to be more religious than men.

Fourth, Davie (1994) suggests that women are more religious than men because of their closer association with birth and death, which are also central issues for many religions:

> My own inclination, however, is to favour those explanations which underline the proximity of women to birth and death ... these ... [by] their very nature, bring to mind questions about the reasons for existence and about the meaning of life ... [the] nature of [women's] religiosity is coloured by such experiences.
>
> (Davie 1994, pp. 120–1)

However we seek to explain the difference in religiosity between women and men, we must also take into account the connections between gender and other social divisions. For example, religiosity changes with age: it tends to peak at both ends of the age spectrum and declines between the ages of twenty-five and fifty. This occurs with women and men, but women start from a higher base level of religiosity and have greater life expectancies. This combination of factors – increased religiosity and greater life expectancy – means that there are more older women than men who believe and practise their religion, just as there are more older women than men in the population as a whole.

Research activity

What is the age profile of your family? Ask any of your family members who are over fifty years of age about their religiosity:

- *Do they attend religious worship?*
- *Why do they attend?*
- *Do they attend more now than when they were younger?*

Gender and the major world religions

Holm and Bowker (1994) note that in almost all the major world religions women are usually subordinate:

> [There is] a contrast between the classical teachings of religions about the equality of men and women and the actual lived experience of women. Expressions that occur frequently include 'inferior', 'polluting', 'male dominated', 'patriarchal'.... Throughout history men have formulated the beliefs of religions, composed and transmitted the sacred writings and been

their sole interpreters, created the religious – and secular – institutions of their societies, and controlled worship and other important rituals.

(Holm and Bowker 1994, p. xiii)

Puttick (1997) agrees:

Women have always been the biggest 'consumers' of religion, but on the whole have been served badly, disparaged and oppressed by the religions themselves. In most … religions, to be born a woman is viewed as a punishment, either for misdeeds in a previous life or for the sin of the first woman: the original Evil temptress … the only recourse is to become a well-behaved, submissive wife and mother in order to be reborn as a man.

(Puttick 1997, p. 1)

It is important for sociologists to be aware of the reasons for this widespread subordination of women in religion. The Christian ritual of thanksgiving after childbirth (often called 'churching') has declined in significance, but it provides clues as to these reasons:

> A month after giving birth, women were welcomed back into the community and restored to their normal social roles by being 'churched', a service which combined thanksgiving with an element of ritual purification.
>
> (Bruce 1996, p. 3)

According to Holm and Bowker (1994) this Christian ritual disguises the belief – widespread throughout Christianity, Islam, Buddhism and Judaism – that women's bodies and women's sexuality are dangerous. As the social anthropologist Mary Douglas (1966) points out, all societies concern themselves with the idea of pollution, especially the 'pollutants' produced by or associated with the body – blood, faeces, disease, for example. This concern is often expressed in religions by means of rules and ceremonies to contain and control pollution. A common stereotype of women is that they are closer than men to the material world of nature because, for example, women menstruate and give birth. They are therefore also likely to be seen as more dangerous and with a greater capacity to pollute religious rituals:

> I believe that some pollutions are used as analogies for expressing a general view of the social order. For example, there are beliefs that each sex is a danger to the other through contact with sexual fluids. According to other beliefs only one sex is endangered by contact with the other, usually males by females .... Such patterns of sexual danger can be seen to express asymmetry or hierarchy .... I suggest that many ideas about sexual dangers are ... mirroring designs of hierarchy ... which apply in the wider social system.
>
> (Douglas 1966, pp. 3–4)

Were religious organizations that developed for, and were run by, women the forerunners of the present day women's movement?

This concern about pollution and the policing of bodies (see below, p. 137) may account for the widespread opposition in many religions to women organizing and officiating at important rituals.

Analyses of religious organizations developed exclusively for women highlight another side to this debate about the extent to which religions disempower women. Holm and Bowker (1994, p. xxi) suggest that religious organizations developed exclusively for women, and controlled and maintained by women (for example, orders of nuns in the Roman Catholic Church), are the forerunners of the modern women's movement. This view takes one of two distinct sociological approaches to such organizations. We can regard them as:

1 a way of separating women from men and, therefore, as part of men's oppression of women;

2 a way of enhancing women's sense of identity; as such, they are an early form of feminism and provide the basis for resistance to the power of men.

Religion, gender, sex and the body

Sexuality is an important issue in many religions. In the Roman Catholic Church, for example, priests are expected to be celibate, while Christianity and Islam (among others) are opposed to gay sexual identities. This concern with sexuality in general means that religions do considerably more than just define roles for women which render them subordinate to men: religions also discipline men. In Turner's (1993) view this disciplinary role in matters concerning sexuality and the body is *central* to religion. The widespread importance in many religions of asceticism – living a life of self-discipline in which the desire for pleasure (especially physical pleasure) does not predominate – is as much to do with policing the body as it is with how, for example, you carry out your priestly duties.

Gay debate the synod bishops do not want

The *Guardian*'s survey of the General Synod members on homosexuality will make awkward reading for the bishops.

Sixty-five per cent of the Church of England's governing body gave the House of Bishops' 1991 report, Issues in Human Sexuality, the thumbs down. The compromise document asserts that active homosexuality can be tolerated among the laity but not among the clergy, but synod says this is not coherent.

Homosexuality is the synod debate the House of Bishops does not want. Its 1991 report has yet to come before synod, and according to the Lesbian and Gay Christian Movement, the synod policy committee has produced an 18-page briefing document about how to keep the matter off the agenda.

Source: *The Guardian*, 8 July 1998

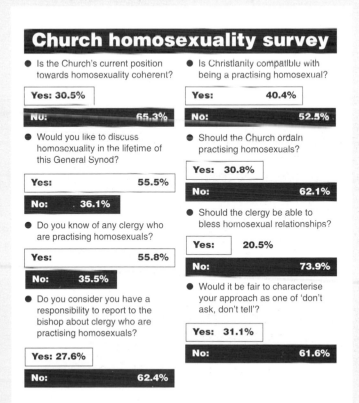

Church homosexuality survey

● Is the Church's current position towards homosexuality coherent?

Yes: 30.5%

No: 65.3%

● Would you like to discuss homosexuality in the lifetime of this General Synod?

Yes: 55.5%

No: 36.1%

● Do you know of any clergy who are practising homosexuals?

Yes: 55.8%

No: 35.5%

● Do you consider you have a responsibility to report to the bishop about clergy who are practising homosexuals?

Yes: 27.6%

No: 62.4%

● Is Christianity compatible with being a practising homosexual?

Yes: 40.4%

No: 52.5%

● Should the Church ordain practising homosexuals?

Yes: 30.8%

No: 62.1%

● Should the clergy be able to bless homosexual relationships?

Yes: 20.5%

No: 73.9%

● Would it be fair to characterise your approach as one of 'don't ask, don't tell'?

Yes: 31.1%

No: 61.6%

Hume says celibacy rule may go

CARDINAL BASIL HUME dramatically intervened in the controversy over the resignation of the bishop who formed a long-standing friendship with a divorcee yesterday by suggesting that the insistence on celibacy for Roman Catholic priests could be changed.

The leader of the Roman Catholic Church in England and Wales said many 'excellent' people were being lost to the Church because of the rule that Catholic priests must remain celibate.

'It is not divine law. It is Church law, so any Pope of General Council could change it,' the cardinal said. 'We are losing excellent and very good people because they would wish to be married priests.'

In his intervention, the cardinal has touched upon an anomaly which allows married former Anglican priests to work alongside Catholic priests who would have liked to marry but could not.

The situation has been created by the growing body of married former Anglican priests who have been accepted into full communion with Rome since the ordination of women by the Church of England.

These number 20 already, with more due to be ordained in Westminster Cathedral next month.

Referendums organised by protest movements in Austria, Germany and France have gathered hundreds of thousands of signatures, with one of their main demands an end to priestly celibacy. In parts of Africa and Latin America, many priests are in relationships.

Source: *The Guardian*, 18 September 1996

Gender, new religious movements and new age movements

Weber (1922b/1978) believed that women are much more important in smaller religious sects than they are in large religious organizations. Bruce's (1996) study of new age movements (NAMs) led him to this conclusion:

> It is a rough-and-ready picture, but, in terms of gender, the New Age divides. The parapsychology and esoteric knowledge side tends to be male. The healing, channelling and spirituality side tends to be female.... Just as in the mainstream churches, women form the majority of the market for the New Age.
>
> (Bruce 1996, p. 220)

What is the major issue for sociologists when they study the links between gender, new religious movements (NRMs) and NAMs?

[This book] asks why well-educated young women with the potential for successful careers and happy home lives ... chose to relegate themselves to the margins in pursuit of spiritual quests.... Did they find or create any improvements over both older religions and secular society?... The main feminist issue in the study of NRMs is gender roles, and the extent to which these movements suppress or liberate women, both spiritually and socially.

(Puttick 1997, p. 5)

Interpretation and evaluation activity

Review what you have learned about NRMs and NAMs and make the case for and against the following:

- *NRMs and NAMs oppress women.*
- *NRMs and NAMs are a form of liberation for women.*

Women and Rastafarianism

Religion's involvement in the oppression or liberation of women is often complex and ambiguous, as can be seen in the case of Rastafarianism. Barrett (1977) and Pryce (1979) suggest that Rastafarianism is a religion that appeals mainly to Afro-Caribbean *men*. Rastafarianism enables men to understand their experience of racial discrimination within a religious framework that also expects women to take on the traditional roles involved in bearing and raising children and making a home. These traditional roles were not available to Afro-Caribbean women during the era of slavery and – according to Rastafarians – they have also been subjected to sexual and racial exploitation ever since. Rasta men believe that traditional female roles protect women from racial and sexual harassment by white society. Rastafarianism is therefore *oppressive* from the point of view of feminist theorists, for example, and *liberatory* from the point of view of Rasta men and women.

Rastafarianism is an example of how there are often no definitive answers to questions about the relationships between religious movements and gender inequalities.

The women who dominate certain aspects of the new age and are the main consumers of new age ideas are predominantly middle class. There is therefore a gender element in the appeal of the new age *and* a class element. Bruce (1996) explains the gender element thus:

More common is the claim that women are essentially if not enormously different ... to men in character because their child-bearing and rearing experiences make them less confrontational, less aggressive, less goal-oriented, less domineering, more co-operative and more caring .... This would certainly fit with the expressive emphasis of the New Age.

(Bruce 1996, pp. 220–1)

Why does the new age appeal predominantly to middle-class women? Very little sociological work has been done in this area, so it is only possible to suggest some answers:

1 Commitment to the new age requires the investment of money and time. This investment is more likely to be feasible for middle-class women than it is for working-class women.

2 Interest in the new age may be related to educational success. Middle-class women are much more likely to have been educated beyond the age of sixteen and to have gained higher qualifications.

3 NAMs are more likely than other religious movements to concern themselves with issues of *psychological* underprivilege (for example, success in one's job and in relationships) rather than *material* underprivilege. Psychological underprivilege is also more likely to be a concern for middle-class women than it is for working-class women.

Gender and fundamentalism

In Chapter 7 (pp. 105–6) we noted that many Christian fundamentalists prescribe a traditional role for women in the family and oppose abortion. To what extent are these views characteristic of religious fundamentalism in general, and why is this the case?

Holm and Bowker (1994) suggests that traditional ideas about women's gender roles are common across all fundamentalisms. He demonstrates that in a wide range of fundamentalist religious movements (including Hindu, Islamic and Christian) women are regarded as subordinate to men and are expected to return to their traditional roles. Even when women play a central role in fundamentalist movements – Hawley (1994) gives the example of a new religious movement in Japan called *Seicho no Ie* – the desire for a return to traditional gender roles remains.

As discussed in Chapter 7 (pp. 103–8) the desire for a return to tradition is a general feature of the fundamentalist response to modernity's emphasis on relativism and individual choice. Why does that return to tradition specifically include a gender element? Why are traditional gender roles so central to fundamentalism?

Fundamentalism develops as a result of the strains and stresses of social change. The general tendency to react to such stresses by strengthening social boundaries also has the effect of strengthening gender boundaries. Fundamentalism attempts to remove the general ambiguities associated with modernity; it removes gender ambiguities by asserting the need for firm gender divisions.

Fundamentalism also seeks a return to a past golden age, even though the past might not have been that golden (see Chapter 7, pp. 105–6). Traditional gender roles are regarded as a constituent element of the golden age, which can guarantee the stability that people believe has been lost with modernity and postmodernity (see Chapter 11). Women, in their traditional place, become the guarantors of a stable future: producing and raising the next generation is a central part of that future.

Hawley (1994) notes that many fundamentalisms are very masculine:

> [There is what] might be called 'religious machismo.... Many fundamentalist groups ... believe that there is a necessity for maleness to reassert itself in the face of a manifest threat. Sikh fundamentalists [for example] tout the martial heroism of Guru Gobind Singh and Maharaja Ranjit Singh ... a Hindu

nationalist group chooses to call itself 'The Army of Shiva'.... Among Christian fundamentalists in the United States, the exhortation 'Onward Christian Soldiers' implies taking a hard line in the fight against Communism.

(Hawley 1994, p. 32)

There are two aspects to this 'machismo' element in fundamentalism: it asserts the central importance of maleness, and it does so by emphasizing the significance of protecting and defending women, who are (or else ought to be) helpless.

In Iran ... sermons preached at the time of the revolution represented onslaughts against the Muslim community (*ummah*) through the metaphor of violations against women, as Muslim men were urged to cast off their weakness in the defence of their 'women' – that is, their community.

(Hawley 1994, p. 33)

This defence of women whose traditional roles re-empower men is also part of the Nation of Islam.

Missionary men

With typical discipline and purpose they marched into the headlines during the Stephen Lawrence enquiry on Monday. They foster black self-esteem and wage a private war on drugs. But they are separatist and believe in black superiority.

The Nation of Islam's origins lie in the flight of Southern blacks to the urban north and the Civil Rights movements of the 1960s – experiences with no equivalent in Britain. The movement began in Detroit in 1930 with a preacher, known by various names including Farrad Mohammad, Wali Farrad, and WD Fard. Fard preached that the true religion of American blacks was that of the blacks of Africa and Asia and made fearless denunciations of whites and Christianity. A hall was hired, renamed the Temple of Islam, and a new movement was born.

The Nation of Islam's approach to its social and political mission is fundamentally different from other black organisations. Historically, black interests in America have been represented by Christian churches and missions with a message of reconciliation and integration. Black Muslims are anti-integrationists. They think that Christianity is a Western conspiracy to keep them forever shackled.

Black Muslims want to redress the balance. After a history of slavery, Congress' unfulfilled promise to recompense blacks who fought in the Civil War, segregation, racist violence, discriminatory hiring policies, underemployment, and a statistically large prison population, they want a fresh start and compensation from America. Originally, they wanted to be repatriated to a new homeland in Africa, but gave up this goal; perhaps when they found themselves winning encouragement from the Ku Klux Klan and other white racists. Today they demand to be given their own state in the US, occupying about a fifth of the country, pro-rata to the size of America's black population.

Supporters of the Nation of Islam are typically young, male, working class, African-American and former Christians, though in recent years, they have also won advance within the college community where traditional teaching has been attacked for its perceived cultural bias (a curriculum typified as 'dead white men').

Source: *The Guardian*, 2 July 1998

The emphasis in the Nation of Islam is on discipline, particularly for men in the face of racial exclusion; there is a strong military flavour with a central security force, the Fruit of Islam. The stress on maleness and reasserting male pride goes hand-in-hand with the assertion that women should return to their traditional role within the family. One lesson for the sociologist is that liberation from oppression is a complex issue: liberation from racial exclusion for black men in the Nation of Islam may lead to further restrictions on women.

Case Study — Women's ordination in the Christian churches

Many religious organizations allow women only a very marginal position; in the Roman Catholic Church, for example, women cannot become priests; in Islam they cannot become imams. This exclusion of women is one reason why feminist theorists regard religion as one of the institutions that maintain male domination; that is, patriarchy.

However, Davie (1994, pp. 179–85) stresses that there are tensions between religion and the wider society. In Britain, for example, women's success in work and education has given them greater access to positions of power, but the Church of England has traditionally excluded women from the priesthood. How does the Church of England respond to the major changes that have occurred in other areas of society?

Women take place at inner sanctum

'She was the best candidate for the job. We are not playing gender politics. She is very good news…
Women should be ordained. I want the best people that we can find.'
John Moses, Dean of St. Paul's

The appointment of the first woman priest to St Paul's Cathedral in London has exposed painful divisions among its clergy, with one of the residential canons declaring that he will not attend when she celebrates communion.

There is no argument that the Rev Lucy Winkett, aged 29, is talented and highly intelligent. A Cambridge history graduate, she joined the Royal College of Music and became a professional singer before the death of her fiancé in a climbing accident caused her to rethink her life. After graduating from Queen's theological college in Birmingham she was ordained as a deacon and then, six months ago as a priest.

Source: *The Guardian*, 13 February 1997

Cleric loses battle against women priests

'I shall pursue this with every fibre of my being'

A priest yesterday became the first churchman to be effectively banned from launching legal actions when the High Court ruled that his one-man campaign against the ordination of women was an abuse of the system.

Two judges declared the Rev Paul Williamson to be a 'vexatious litigant', which means he loses the automatic right to sue without the court's prior permission.

The court heard that Mr Williamson, of Feltham, Middlesex, had started at least 14 separate cases against the Church of England for ordaining women – including suing the Archbishops of Canterbury and York for treason. Despite constant defeats and warnings by judges, he had continued launching actions.

Lord Justice Rose said: 'I have no hesitation in concluding that he has habitually and persistently and without any reasonable ground instituted vexatious proceedings.

Source: *The Guardian*, 17 July 1997

From 1992 the Church of England allowed the ordination of women to the priesthood. The reasons for this change in policy are of interest to sociologists. Beginning in 1970, decisions over doctrinal matters and the appointment of bishops passed to the Church of England's General Synod (prior to 1970 the prime minister appointed bishops). The General Synod is the Church of England's governing body. It comprises three 'houses': the House of Bishops, the House of Clergy and the House of Laity. In the 1980s the General Synod agreed in principle that women could be ordained as priests if they were already deacons of the church. Only in 1994, however, were the first women ordained as priests. This enabled them to perform all the religious rituals previously monopolized by men, including marriages, funerals and baptisms.

The debate about the ordination of women to the priesthood has a number of features of sociological interest:

1 Some Christian churches already had women clergy (for example, Methodists, Presbyterians and Pentecostalists) and this seems not to have concerned those who were affiliated to those religions.

2 There was mixed support for women's ordination within the Church of England itself, with the laity least in favour.
3 The issue of lay support posed difficulties for the hierarchy of the Church of England. If the church as a whole supported the ordination of women to the priesthood, how could its decision be imposed on those who opposed ordination? (The church lacked both the power and the authority to do this.)
4 Point (3) leads to a divided church with fundamental disagreement about a major theological issue.
5 Women's ordination to the priesthood has placed severe limitations on ecumenicalism, in that the Roman Catholic Church remains opposed to the ordination of women.

Many of these points relate to issues discussed in Chapters 6 and 7. If a religious organization responds to changes in the wider society – in this case, to the general opening up of opportunities for women – does this compromise suggest that the organization is becoming more secular?

St Paul's faithful walk out in row over woman priest

A full-time priest at St Paul's is set to resign in a bitter row over the appointment of a female canon to the cathedral's staff.

Other resignations would follow if the Rev Lucy Winkett takes up her post in the autumn. Traditionalist priests in the London diocese – where St Paul's is the mother church – are already threatening to boycott services at the cathedral; they may establish an alternative power base.

The controversy over Winkett's appointment as the cathedral's first woman priest threatens to become the Church of England's most acrimonious dispute since legislation allowing the ordination of women was passed five years ago.

Source: *The Sunday Times*, 11 May 1997

Case Study / Women and Islam

Stereotypes of Islam and what Edward Said calls 'Orientalism' (see Chapter 6, pp. 84–5) include assumptions about Muslim women and emphasize the exploitative nature of Muslim families, which are thought to be dominated by men. It is believed that women are forced to dress in a particular way, to veil their faces when in public and are not allowed to choose their own marriage partners.

Studies by Watson (1994) and Butler (1995) suggest that these beliefs are not accurate for Muslim women living in Britain and for those living in countries where Islam is the dominant religion. Watson and Butler take up issues raised by Anwar (1981) relating to how Asian immigrants to Britain adapted to British culture.

Anwar describes major differences between the first generation of migrants and their children. For the first generation who arrived in Britain in the 1960s, the main issue was how to build a Pakistani or Bangladeshi life in Britain. The religious traditions of Islam became the basis for building such a life and gave Muslim people a sense of community and identity. The second generation, born in Britain, is caught between two cultures. Three issues are central to the relationship between the two

generations: arranged marriages, Western clothes and freedom of decision-making. These three issues had a particular impact on women. The first generation saw women as the future of their community – as child-bearers and religious socializers – and was concerned that second-generation, Muslim women were moving away from their traditions. The women themselves saw this as part of their freedom in a new culture.

Butler's (1995) study develops and revises Anwar's. On the basis of interviews conducted with groups of Asian women and men, Butler identifies a recognition that traditional ways of life are breaking down (for example, more Asian women are entering the professions), but that religion is still important:

> Asian Muslim women in Britain are seeking new roles for themselves, ones that give them more independence and choice, yet, at the same time, supporting and strengthening their commitment is Islam ....
>
> Whatever other cultural systems have to offer, none are considered to be as important or as encompassing as those of Islam. Thus, for second generation Asian Muslim women, Islam represents the major guide to life with which they construct their individual identities and lifestyles.
>
> (Butler 1995, p. 21)

These views challenge the stereotype of Islam as oppressive towards women:

> It was custom that encouraged women to be obedient to their husbands and not to show disrespect. Such restrictions were not laid down in the Qur'an.
>
> (Butler 1995, p. 20)

Watson's (1994) study of veiling describes a similar misunderstanding of Islam and an unawareness that religion does not necessarily oppress women. As one of Watson's interviewees put it:

> There are lots of other advantages to wearing the veil ... I find it easier to mix and get around in public and not to be bothered by lecherous stares or worse. But these are just advantages of a certain style of dress which doesn't draw attention to the body or fit the Western stereotype of sexy clothes. They don't have anything specific to do with Islam, they have more to do with being female in a sexist and male-dominated society.
>
> (Watson 1994, p. 149)

The veil is therefore much more than solely a religious issue. It also allows women to cope with what they see as the dangers of a sexist society. They can wear the veil without any implication that they are committed Muslims.

Conclusion

A major part of the debate about religion and gender is concerned with the extent to which religion is part of the maintenance of patriarchy. Walby's (1992) discussion of the structures of patriarchy indicates what it is about religions that might predispose them to support gender inequalities:

Structures of patriarchy	Patriarchal aspects of religion
Household	Stress, in many world religions, on the family, marriage and monogamy.
Employment	Women's exclusion from important roles in many churches.
The state	Where church organizations are linked to the state, they generally support women's family role.
Culture	Idealization of traditional ideas about femininity in many world religions.
Sexuality	Emphasis, in many religions, on the control of women's sexuality.

There is certainly nothing inevitable about religions in general oppressing women, but in practice many religions do oppress women.

Essay question

How far do religious organizations and religious beliefs maintain those systems of inequality which disadvantage women?

Coursework suggestion

There is very little sociological work on the relationship between gender and religion. However, there are opportunities for interesting coursework that looks at this relationship. You could observe a religious service and see what roles women perform. To what extent do those roles relate to patriarchy?

You could also study a particular religious organization. Does it suggest traditional roles for women? Does it, for example, oppose women's widespread entry into the labour market?

You could also study the images of women and men in the literature of any religion in which you are interested. How are women and men represented? Are those representations traditional? Are they likely to oppress women?

DIRECT RESPONSE QUESTIONS
Item 1

Female deities are quite often found in religions across the world. These are sometimes thought of as 'womanly', gentle and loving; in other instances, goddesses appear as fearful destroyers. Women warrior gods, for example are found fairly often, even though in actual social life women are only very occasionally military leaders...there seems to be few if any religions in which females are the dominant figures, either symbolically or as religious authorities ... The Christian religion was born of what was in a fundamental sense a revolutionary movement; but in their attitudes towards women, some of the major Christian churches are among the most conservative organisations in modern societies. Women ministers have long been accepted in some sects and denominations, but the Catholic and Anglican churches persisted in formally supporting inequalities of gender.

(Giddens, A, 1997, *Sociology*, Cambridge, Polity Press, 450 and 452)

Item 2

... the New Age rests on the premise that the self is basically good and that problems stem from its being confirmed by institutional roles. In that sense, the critique of gender roles that is at least implicit in New Age thought is even more far-reaching than that of much feminist literature. It is not only the present patriarchal roles which need to be challenged. Rather it is the whole practice of encouraging people to interact on the basis of role which must be replaced by authenticity ... New Age reorientation ... [effects] the private world of personal relationships. Although there are 'new men' who are attracted to the idea of changing gender roles, it is obvious that any restructuring will have greater appeal to the group most likely to benefit from the change – that is, to women.

(Bruce, 1997: 221)

1 In the first item, what are the difference in attitudes to women of Christian churches and others sects and denominations?

2 In the second item, what are the main differences in attendance at worship between (a) daughters and sons; and (b) between age/generational groups?

3 What is the appeal of the New Age to women? How far is that not the appeal of mainstream religions?

4 What are the main reasons why women appear to be more religious than men? Do these suggest that the process of secularisation, if it is occurring, is gendered?

References and further reading

Anwar, M. (1981) *Between Two Cultures: A study of relationships between generations in the Asian Community in Britain*, London: Commission for Racial Equality.

Barrett, L. (1977) *The Rastafarians: The dreadlocks of Jamaica*, Kingston (Jamaica): Sangster Books.

Bruce, S. (1996) *Religion in the Modern World: From cathedrals to cults*, Oxford: Oxford University Press.

Butler, C. (1995) 'Religion and gender: young Muslim women in Britain', *Sociology Review*, 4:2, pp. 18–22.

Davie, G. (1994) *Religion in Britain since 1945: Believing without belonging*, Oxford: Blackwell.

Douglas, M. (1966) *Purity and Prayer*, London: Routledge.

Hawley, J.S. (1994) *Fundamentalism and Gender*, Oxford: Oxford University Press.

Holm, J. and Bowker, T. (1994) *Women in religion*, London: Pinter Publishers.

Jacobs, E. and Worcester, R. (1994) *Britain under the MORI-scope*, London: Wiedenfeld and Nicholson.

Pryce, K. (1979) *Endless Pressure: A study of West Indian lifestyles in Bristol*, Harmondsworth: Penguin.

Puttick, K. (1997) *Women in New Religions: In search of community, sexuality and spiritual power*, London: Sage.

Sharma, A. (1987) *Women in World Religion*, Albany: State University of New York Press.

Turner, B. (1993) *Religion and Social Theory*, London: Sage.

Walby, S. (1992) *Theorising Patriarchy*, Oxford: Blackwell.

Walker, A. (1990) 'Why are most churchgoers women?', *Vox Evangelica*, 20, pp. 73–90.

Watson, H. (1994) 'Women and the veil: personal responses to global process', in A.S. Ahmed and H. Donnan, *Islam, globalization and postmodernity*, London: Routledge, pp. 141–59.

Weber, M. (1922b/1978) 'The soteriology of the underprivileged', in W.G. Runciman, *Max Weber: Selections in translation*, Cambridge: Cambridge University Press, pp.174–91.

Religion and social change

Key terms	Key thinkers
Social change	Karl Marx
Social structure	Max Weber
Charisma	Emile Durkheim
Chiliasm of despair	Elie Halevy
Millenarianism	Edward Thompson
Millennialism	Norman Cohn
Materialism	Michael Adas
Idealism	Peter Worsley

Introduction

We have already seen some examples of the relationships between religion and processes of **social change**; religious fundamentalism (Chapter 7, pp. 103–6); the moral conservatism of the Christian Right in the USA (Chapter 7, pp. 97–101); the role of religion in Northern Ireland (Chapter 8, pp. 126–8); the extent to which religion is part of the patriarchal domination of women (Chapter 9, pp. 131–2). This chapter will extend some of these examples and will also discuss what sociologists *mean* when they talk about social change. It will contrast those theories which regard religion as a basically conservative force that inhibits social change (linked to what Marx said about the social role of religion and to the views of many sociological functionalists – see Chapter 2, pp. 16–17) with those theories which regard religion as having the potential to lead to social change (linked to Weber's discussion of the relationships between modern capitalist societies and religion – see pp. 150–3). We will also look at some of the work of historians (E.P. Thompson, for example) who have studied the role that religion played in the development of the working class in the nineteenth century; and the work of social anthropologists who have studied the role of religion in small-scale societies experiencing their first contacts with modern societies.

Social change

Interpretation activity

What do you understand by the term 'social change'? Take five minutes to brainstorm lots of examples of social change. What do these examples have in common?

Sociology developed at a time of profound social change when complex, modern industrial societies arose in the late eighteenth and nineteenth centuries. Much of the work of the founders of sociology – especially that of Marx, Weber and Durkheim –discussed the nature and effects of these changes. We can gain some idea of what the founders of sociology meant by social change by contrasting their views on premodern and modern societies.

	Premodern	**Modern**
Marx	Feudalism	Capitalism
	Rural, peasant society	Urban, industrial society
	Private ownership of land	Private ownership of industrial capital
Weber	Peasant society	Capitalism
	Rural society	Urban society
	Tradition	Bureaucracy (see Chapter 4, p. 45)
Durkheim	Simple society	Complex society
	Simple division of labour	Elaborate division of labour
	Mechanical solidarity (see Chapter 2, p. 22)	Organic solidarity (see Chapter 1, p. 22)
	One system of values and ideas	Many systems of values and ideas

All these thinkers agree that modern societies came into being as a result of major changes in the **social structure** – that is, the way that people live together and organize their lives. According to Durkheim, the division of labour became more complex and more people specialized in doing a single task; according to Marx, the whole social class structure changed from one dominated by landowners and peasants to one dominated by large industrial employers and their workers; according to Weber, a society dominated by tradition became one dominated by rational calculations as to the best way of doing things. In addition, there were major changes in *where* and *how* people lived: from rural to urban living, from large families to smaller families; and major changes in the sorts of *institutions* in which most people worked – large bureaucracies rather than small farms, for example.

Social change, therefore, implies change to a whole social system, but there is clearly more to it than that. After all, there are always changes in the way we live our lives: for example, changes in the world economic system require people to change the way they spend their money; changes in government policy can change relationships between men and women. This suggests that:

● we live in a society where change is continuous;

● there is more to social change than the major structural changes analysed by the founders of sociology.

We can say, therefore, that sociologists are interested in two kinds of social change: first, change to a *whole* society and, second, change *within* a society. The first kind of social change is likely to be more dramatic in its effects.

Interpretation activity

Look back at your examples of social change in the activity on p. 147. Which of them are:

● *changes to a whole society?*
● *changes within a society?*

Religion and social change

Much sociological work on the relationships between religion and social change has looked at the impact of religion on major structural changes; for example, the move from premodern to modern societies. We saw in Chapter 2 how some of the founders of sociology – Marx, for example – regard religion as an opiate which tends to inhibit social change (see pp. 16–17). Conversely, we also saw how Weber is less convinced about the conservative effects of religious activity. As Weber suggests (see Chapter 4, pp. 45–7), some religious organizations – those called churches – tend to support the status quo, while others – religious sects – are more likely to challenge the status quo. This makes some religious organizations potentially radical and thus more likely to promote social change than to inhibit it.

By contrasting the views of Marx and Weber we will see how their ideas have influenced later sociologists and historians. Some have argued that religion prevents social change, others that it can effect change, and still others that the same religions can be conservative or radical in their effects, depending upon their context.

Marx and religion as a conservative force

Karl Marx argued that religion is an opiate for the disaffected masses.

In Chapter 2 (pp. 16–17) we saw how Marx argued that religion is an opiate: that is, a system of beliefs and practices which conceals from people the real circumstances in which they live. Marx viewed all societies as based on social class divisions and systems of class inequality. These class inequalities produce inequalities in income, wealth and property ownership. It is these inequalities which religion either conceals or justifies.

> **Research and evaluation activity**
>
> *Look back at the section on Marx in Chapter 2, pp. 16–17 According to Marx, how do religious beliefs justify the existence of social inequality?*

It is the ability of religion to justify social inequality, to make it seem a natural, and therefore acceptable, part of society, which makes religion an opiate. In *justifying* social inequality, religion prevents people from *challenging* social inequality. Religion is therefore a conservative force in society.

It is important to realize that, for Marx, the presence of religion is not the only thing that inhibits social change. There are, for example, other ideologies that have a similar effect, among them the belief that a democratic political system is responsive to the needs of those who are disadvantaged. There are also other social institutions that are conservative in their consequences. According to many Marxists, the education system is conservative because it educates people to fit into social positions – different jobs and occupations – which reward people very unequally.

If, as Marx argues, religion prevents social change, then what is it that makes social change more likely? For Marx, the answer is fairly straightforward. Change is likely to occur when there are two sets of conditions. First, a set of structural conditions in which, for example, the economic system is in crisis – high inflation, high unemployment, rising poverty. Second, a group of people – in Marx's argument, sections of the working class who do not own property and capital – who realize that there is a crisis and who organize themselves politically and economically to challenge the existing system. Marx's view of social change is, therefore, a revolutionary one: social change occurs through significant social conflict in which social classes are opposed to each other. The success of one social class – in obtaining a redistribution of property, for example – can only occur at a cost to another social class – the one that owned the property in the past. The only role for religion in this process is to inhibit the likelihood that people will be aware that there is a social crisis and inhibit any idea that people themselves can intervene to tackle that crisis. Religion is, therefore, an ideology which generates forms of **false consciousness**: that is, it promotes false ideas about how society works and about how people can cope with social inequality. These ideas will not really abolish inequality.

Evaluation activity

In Chapters 6 and 7 we looked at some examples of how religious people directly criticized the policies of elected governments (see, for instance, Chapter 6, pp. 89–92, and Chapter 7, pp. 98–101). Do these examples invalidate Marx's claim that religion is a conservative force? Give reasons for your answers.

Weber and relationships between religion and capitalist development

Max Weber asserted that religion could be a force for social change.

Marx's approach set the agenda for the sociological debate about the role of religion in processes of social change. We will now look at Weber's challenge to Marx's views.

There are three elements to Weber's work on the sociology of religion which are important for our purposes: first, Weber's analysis of the relationships between religion and the development of capitalism; second, his studies of world religions – in particular, Confucianism and Hinduism – and how these might have inhibited the development of capitalism; third, his studies of charisma and its importance in initiating processes of social change.

The 'Weber thesis': Protestantism and capitalism

Weber is interested in the role of religion in processes of social change. Whereas Marx views the causes of social change as *structural* – technology, the distribution of wealth, how people make their living – Weber is convinced that *ideas* themselves are important. According to Weber, ideas do not just *result* from major social changes; they may help *initiate* those processes.

Materialism and idealism

We can broadly distinguish two sorts of explanation of social change and the relative importance they ascribe to structural factors and ideas. One sort of explanation argues that the really significant factors are *structural* ones. This is Marx's view as a **materialist**; ideas are a product of social change and certain religious ideas are produced by certain social structures. For Marx, Protestant religious ideas are the product of a capitalist social structure.

The other sort of explanation – and the alternative to the materialist view – argues that *ideas* produce social change; social groups can have an idea about a better society – one that reduces social inequality, for example – and then bring this society into existence. This sort of ➤

explanation can be called **idealist**, not because the people are idealists but because of the formative role given to ideas themselves. As we will see later (pp. 151–5), Weber tries to avoid both these extremes by arguing that processes of social change involve structural changes *and* changes in ideas, without one causing the other.

Put simply, Weber looks at the role religion plays in social change because few thinkers before him had taken seriously the idea that religion might be a radical force rather than a conservative one.

Weber's approach is indicated by the title of one of his books – *The Protestant Ethic and the Spirit of Capitalism* – published in 1904. There are three elements to Weber's discussion of the relationships between religion and capitalism: what he calls the 'spirit of capitalism'; the Protestant ethic, which derives from the theologian Martin Luther; and ideas about religious salvation, which derive from the work of another theologian, John Calvin. It is the combination of these three elements which led Weber to conclude that certain religious beliefs and practices played a crucial role in capitalist development, and to offer an explanation of why some parts of Europe and the United States were more progressive than others and were, in consequence, the first to develop capitalism.

Martin Luther argued that all legitimate activity was God-given.

It is important to emphasize that Weber and Marx appear to agree about what capitalism is: they both stress the importance of private property, profit and rates of interest, large-scale factory production, money economies and banking, and cities. However, Weber is much more interested than Marx in 'the spirit of capitalism': that is, the ideas, values and motivations that drove people to become capitalists.

The spirit of capitalism is close to what many people now take for granted and is, for example, the basis of the banking system: hard work, investment, the avoidance of waste and indulgence, and a careful use of money and other economic resources.

According to Weber, this set of motivations is not characteristic of many premodern societies; it is, however, characteristic of societies that, in the seventeenth and eighteenth centuries in particular, were beginning to develop capitalism. This leaves Weber with two questions: 'Where did this ethic come from?' and 'Why do many people live their lives in accordance with this ethic?' For Weber, the answers to both these questions lie in religious ideas that were themselves new and revolutionary in their theological impact.

According to Weber's analysis, the Protestant ethic derives from the work of Martin Luther (1483–1547) and some of the ideas of John Calvin (1509–64) on predestination. This analysis leads Weber to link religion and capitalist development.

Ideas and time

Important issues about time sequences are crucial to Weber's argument. Luther and Calvin lived and worked in the sixteenth century, before the development of capitalism. The religious and theological issues important to Luther and Calvin predate capitalism and were solely debates within theology about the nature of God, prayer, the Bible, etc. Later, these ideas came to have a wider social and economic significance. Critically, this means that the ideas were not a *result* of capitalist development but were there *already*, to be taken up by capitalist entrepreneurs as a justification for their activities.

Luther himself was not really interested in the role of religious ideas in economic life; his interests were mainly theological and concerned his Protestant disagreements with the Roman Catholic Church. In particular, whereas Roman Catholicism distinguished between sacred and secular activity and regarded the former as more important in the eyes of God, Luther argued that all legitimate activity was God-given and therefore of equal value. This meant that going to church on Sunday, for example, was no more religious than any other activity, such as working hard in your job, which is also a calling from God. Such work, however, had to be carried out with the seriousness that any God-given activity requires.

This provides a link with the spirit of capitalism. This spirit – hard, serious work – receives a religious justification in the form of the Protestant ethic. Both require what Weber calls *asceticism*, as indicated in the following example of Protestant theology:

> Waste of time is thus the first and in principle the deadliest of sins. The span of human life is infinitely short and precious to make sure of one's own election [to the ranks of those who are to be saved] .... Loss of time through sociability, idle talk, luxury, even more sleep than is necessary ... is worthy of absolute moral condemnation .... [Time] is infinitely valuable because every hour lost is lost to labour for the glory of God.
>
> (Weber 1904/1974, p. 158)

Notice what Weber suggests: religious ideas – developed purely for religious reasons – come to have effects way beyond the religious sphere; in this case, effects on economic activity. As Weber puts it, there is an 'elective affinity' between a religious ethic and a form of economic activity. Religion played a significant role in the major social changes that brought the modern world into being.

The third element in Weber's analysis pertains to some of John Calvin's ideas about how people are saved by God and their fate after death. Calvin, like Luther, argued about theological issues with the Roman Catholic Church. His major point of contention with Catholicism was its claim that people could know that they are saved and go to heaven, and that if they believed themselves to be damned, they could nevertheless obtain salvation through religious activity, such as prayer and confession. Calvin, in common with other Protestant theologians, believed that this was an error. Calvin argued that people were predestined to heaven or hell; God decided at the birth of each individual if they were to be saved or damned. Religious activity of any kind could not change this decision. Of course, this belief severely limits the traditional role of the church because no amount of prayer by believers or clergy makes any difference. In Weber's view, Calvinism poses profound problems for believers: if I am damned and can do nothing about it, then what is life for? Why should I do anything at all? Why should I be religious?

John Calvin believed that people were predestined to heaven or hell.

Weber describes the psychological condition of Calvinists as one of inner loneliness. They dealt with this situation – which is potentially negative – in two related ways. First, it became one of their duties in life to believe that they would be saved; second, working hard in intense worldly activity – economic activity – became a sign to others that they would be saved. This then links with the Protestant ethic and the spirit of capitalism to further encourage intense, ascetic, worldly activity on the part of religious people. The Protestant ethic and ideas about predestination do not just allow people to *accept* the spirit of capitalism; they *promote* that spirit by giving it a profound religious significance. The religious ideas of Calvin and Luther, developed in the fifteenth and sixteenth centuries, encouraged people in the seventeenth and eighteenth centuries to master and take control of the world – they are what Weber calls *this-worldly* ideas. Such ideas deny the validity, for example, of withdrawal from the world into a monastery.

Research and evaluation activity

What are Weber's main reasons for arguing that religions played a significant part in the development of capitalism? Do you find his argument convincing?

Weber and the sociology of world religions

On the basis of the argument described above, Weber is able to identify those parts of Europe – England, Scotland, Holland – and North America which are Lutheran and Calvinist as the most economically progressive and as the first to develop capitalism. Conversely, Roman Catholic areas – Italy, Spain – are noticeably late in developing capitalism. Weber therefore answers the question 'Is religion a force for social change?' in the affirmative. In Protestant areas of Europe and North America, religion enhanced the development of capitalism. We will discuss later the extent to which Weber argues that religion *caused* the development of capitalism.

Weber extended this analysis in his studies of some of the major world religions, in particular Confucianism and Hinduism. His argument is that China and India, for example, had many of the features characteristic of modern capitalist societies – money economies, cities, bureaucracies. In both countries, these predated the emergence of such features in Western Europe and North America. However, the religious ethics of Confucianism in China and Hinduism in India were very different to Protestantism. Whereas the implication of Protestantism was for people to take control of their destinies and of the world, Confucianism encouraged *adjustment* to the world as it is, while Hinduism recommended *withdrawal* from the world as the only truly religious attitude. These are all perfectly understandable religious ethics, but only Protestantism favoured the development of capitalism.

In these ways, Weber offers an explanation of the relationship between religion and social change which is neither materialist nor idealist; changes in social structure did not produce the theological innovations of Luther and Calvin, nor did those changes produce the spirit of capitalism. The relevant theological innovations were certainly in existence well before the development of capitalism, but they only became significant for how people understood their economic lives when the structural conditions were right.

Weber does not claim that Protestantism *caused* capitalism, for two reasons. First, he does not think that the sort of causal explanations physicists and chemists provide can be used to explain social life; something like the development of capitalism will have a large number of causes. Second, a religious ethic develops for particular reasons that have little to do with wider social issues, like economic behaviour. Only later does a religious ethic take on a wider significance.

Although Weber argues that religion played an important part in the development of capitalism, he also argues that once capitalism is established, the religious ethic becomes less and less important. In addition, capitalism can then develop in other societies without the existence of that religious ethic. Thus, capitalist societies now exist in the context of many different religious ethics – in Italy, in Russia, in Iran, in Japan. None of these are countries in which Protestantism has any major significance.

Charisma and social change

We discussed Weber's concept of **charisma** in Chapter 4 (pp. 50–3) in relation to sects and other religious organizations. Charisma is also significant in Weber's work, as one of the major causes of social change. We can examine Weber's argument in the context of religious organizations.

We saw in Chapter 4 (pp. 45–6) how the religious organizations sociologists call churches are likely to support the status quo. They are therefore likely to represent those groups that are more powerful and have greater status. In other words, churches can find it difficult to represent underprivileged people, such as the poor and the unemployed. This is why Weber regards religious sects as the kind of religious organization with most appeal to the underprivileged.

Charisma provides a basis for sectarian breakaways from churches. As we saw in Chapter 4 (p. 50–2), in order for a religious sect to develop in opposition to a church there has to exist a social group whose needs are not satisfied by their church, led by a charismatic individual who claims to be able to satisfy those needs. Social change is therefore partly dependent on a charismatic breakaway from an established organization. Such a breakaway can be from an established church; alternatively, it can also come from a dominant political organization or party.

Weber regards a charismatic breakaway as unstable, in particular, because it is possible for it to fail and because the leader – with his or her unique characteristics – inevitably dies. Charisma therefore has to be *routinized*: it has to be built into social structures that will live on after the death of the charismatic leader. This routinization can take two forms. One form develops traditional ways of deciding who the next leader should be, or who will control the movement – by heredity, for example, which can ensure that a relative of the leader will succeed. The other form develops what is effectively a more modern routinization – a new leader may have to meet formal criteria for gaining power, such as recognized qualifications and experience. In both these forms of routinization the original character of charisma – its revolutionary potential, its magical qualities – are watered down.

Research activity

Try to identify two examples of charismatic breakaways in political movements.

Weber's analysis of the importance of religion in the development of capitalism has been taken up by historians studying eighteenth- and nineteenth-century Britain. Two of the most important are Elie Halevy and Edward Thompson.

Halevy: why there was no political revolution in Britain

France in the eighteenth century and Russia in the twentieth century had major political revolutions which were violent and which initiated major structural changes in the economy, in politics and in cultural life. Halevy (1924, 1927) noted that Britain had no equivalent political revolution; that capitalism developed in Britain without major political upheaval and struggle. Halevy argued that this was largely the result of religious practice and belief. Religion does not inhibit change, but it does affect how change comes about.

Halevy is principally interested in the role of one particular religious movement: Methodism. Methodism was established by John Wesley in the eighteenth century in opposition to the conservatism of the established Church of England and to more radical, non-conformist movements. Methodism is important for Halevy because of the role it plays in the development of labour movements and trades unions. Many of the leaders of early trades unions were committed Methodists. Methodism is also important because it had a significant part in the development of a middle class of business people that was very different from the aristocracy and landowning classes. Whereas the latter were Church of England, many of the former started as supporters of radical, non-conformist movements and subsequently became

Methodists. This change of religious ethic enabled their upward mobility into the ranks of the ruling class (if they continued to support more radical religious movements this would not have occurred). Therefore, Methodism prevented the more radical and violent changes in the class structure that happened during the French Revolution of the late eighteenth and nineteenth centuries.

Non-conformist religions

Methodism is one of many non-conformist movements, which also include Baptists, Quakers and the Salvation Army. Non-conformism has a long history going back to the Act of Uniformity in 1662, which demanded strict observance of the teachings of the Church of England and of the Book of Common Prayer. Non-conformists, as the name suggests, reject those teachings in one way or another. The name Methodism derives from the methodical and careful way in which Methodists study the Bible.

Methodist Central Hall, Westminster.

Edward Thompson: Methodism and the working classes

Halevy studied the expansion of Methodism in the eighteenth century and saw that its major support was among those who were becoming owners of industrial enterprises and members of the ruling class, and thus more politically powerful. Thompson noted that support for Methodism in the nineteenth century among the working class increased dramatically. Allowing for the difficulties in measuring such support, it is estimated that Methodism had 60,000 adherents in the 1780s and 248,000 adherents in 1830; many of these were industrial workers. Why was this?

Thompson offers three reasons. First, there were ways in which people were indoctrinated into Methodism, among which was a thriving Sunday school movement in working-class areas. Second, Methodism provided more than religious ideas alone; it also stressed the importance of community and people helping each other. This was significant in a period of rapid social change and dislocation, in which many traditional communities had been destroyed. Third, Methodism gained a lot of support after revolutionary expectations – partly resulting from the revolutionary insurrections in France – had not been met. Thompson describes these processes as involving a **chiliasm of despair**, an emotional and ecstatic reaction to failed political aspirations and to profound social changes which could not be accommodated in the established Church of England.

Research and evaluation activity

Summarize in 250 words Halevy's and Thompson's views about the part religion played in the development of capitalism in the United Kingdom and the part Methodism played in political change.

Millenarianism and millennialism

Thompson strongly suggests that some forms of religion are a reaction to periods of profound social change and unmet political aspirations: when political activity fails, religious activity takes its place. Social dislocation and the failure of political movements have been identified as significant issues in contemporary premodern societies experiencing the challenges of contact with modern societies, and in reactions to colonialism and imperialism.

Norman Cohn (1970) studying Europe, Michael Adas (1979) studying British colonies in the nineteenth and early twentieth centuries, and Peter Worsley (1968) studying cargo cults in contemporary premodern societies, all regard processes of social change as critical in explaining the emergence of millenarian movements; that is, movements which see the possibility of total, imminent salvation through the adoption of a particular religious message.

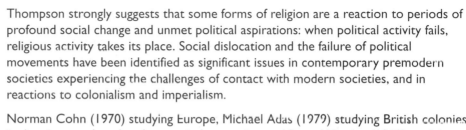

Salvation now

Sociologists and historians use a number of terms to describe movements that believe in imminent, total salvation. In particular, they use the terms **millenarian** and **millennial**. These two terms label identical movements. In the rest of this chapter we will use the terms **millenarian** and **millenarianism**.

Cohn's (1970) *Pursuit of the Millennium* studies a wide range of European millenarian movements in the Middle Ages. These movements have a number of features in common. First, they viewed salvation as imminent, total and collective, and that it would happen here on earth via miraculous, perhaps divine, intervention. Second, they gave a central role to a prophet who represented the main adherents of such movements, the underprivileged. Third, millenarian movements developed when political movements for social change had failed, and especially when they had been persecuted by the authorities. For example, the Hussites in fifteenth-century Bohemia were initially a political movement, led by Jan Huss, with a limited set of political objectives aimed at the poor. When their activities were ruthlessly suppressed by the Bohemian authorities, the Hussites saw themselves as a persecuted group and the movement became more religious and millenarian.

Michael Adas's (1979) study begins with an example that summarizes many of the issues raised by religion in situations of profound social change and dislocation:

> Near the town of Dedaye in Lower Burma in January 1931, a well-armed party of colonial police was confronted by an irregular mass of nearly seven hundred Burman peasants ... the peasants, armed only with knives, spears and a few antique firearms, advanced fearlessly across open ground toward the ready guns of the Indian and Burmese [troops]. As they marched, the leaders of the rebel throng chanted cabalistic incantations to stupefy the enemy troops and rang sacred gongs to render their adversaries' rifles and machine guns useless. The rank-and-file clutched protective talismans ... and displayed magic symbols tattooed to their chests and arms, which were intended to confer invulnerability. The peasants did not hesitate because their victory seemed certain. All signs indicated that the forces of the cosmos were on their side. Many believed that Saya San, the prophet who had exhorted them to rebellion, was the coming Buddha or the Buddha's messenger. He had promised an end to the infidels' rule and restoration of the Burman monarchy and the Buddhist religion. Through their prophet leader, the peasants sought to usher in a golden age of harmony and prosperity ... the [troops] opened fire. Nearly two hours later the bewildered remnants of the rebel force withdrew leaving hundreds of their comrades dead or wounded on the field of battle.
>
> (Adas 1979, p. xvii)

This example has all the features of a millenarian movement: the experience of colonialism and the rapid social changes that this involved; a religious prophet who claims to be able to challenge oppression and initiate a golden age in which traditions are re-established; followers who use religious ideas and religious objects to oppose the forces of oppression; finally, failure.

Evaluation activity

Why do you think many millenarian movements fail in their attempt to resist the social dislocations that accompany social change?

Peter Worsley (1968) and a number of social anthropologists are interested in millenarian movements in traditional premodern societies, and how such movements help people cope with some of the problems brought by contact with modern capitalist societies. As with the movements studied by Norman Cohn (1970), these millenarian movements recruit support from among the underprivileged and are potentially revolutionary because they reject the dominant values of society. They often take a religious form because of the importance of religion in many premodern societies. Their religious elements are very like those identified by Cohn. There is an expectation that salvation – often seen in terms of the benefits of modernity: wealth, money, material possessions – will arrive in the very near future for those who follow the leader of the movement. As with all millenarian movements, there are major problems predicting an imminent and earthly salvation: if salvation does not come, then what is the movement to do? In essence, millenarian movements react to the non-arrival of the predicted salvation either by splitting into a number of separate movements or by disappearing altogether.

Conclusion

We can summarize the sociological debate about social change as follows. There is disagreement between those who see religion as a conservative force and those who see it as actually or potentially radical. This disagreement originates in the contrasting views of Marx and Weber. Most scholars who have developed the arguments of Marx and Weber are historians interested in the formative period of modernity, in the eighteenth and early nineteenth centuries. Although there is no consensus about who is right, it is generally agreed that religion can have a range of effects on social change. Sometimes, religion is regarded as having both radical and conservative effects. In Halevy's argument, for example, religion is important for the development of an industrial middle class in Britain – that is, it aids social change – but religion enables that change to happen without violent political revolution – that is, it has some conservative effects.

Case Study — Islam and modernity

The mixture of radical and conservative potentials within religion can be illustrated in a case study of the Islamic Revolution in Iran in 1979. This revolution replaced a political leader (the Shah of Iran) with a religious leader (Ayatollah Khomeini) and instituted a political and economic system in which religion was central. What exactly was the role of religion in the revolution? Was it an important contributory factor to the major changes that occurred in Iran at the end of the 1970s?

Two issues stand out which are important for assessing the role that religion plays in any processes of social change. First, the revolution in Iran was a particular kind of revolution, a revolution against forms of imperialism; in this case, it involved the USA's domination of the Iranian economy and fear among some Iranians that this domination extended to cultural and political life, including religion. Second, Islam in Iran became a central focus of the revolution, whose leader was a cleric, the Ayatollah Khomeini.

Islam was especially important in the revolution because of its part in political life. Islam, particularly the movement called Shi'a Islam, does not separate the political from the religious and gives religious leaders a central role in political life. Not only is it the role of the state to allow Islam to flourish, the state itself should be run on Islamic principles and organized according to the principles of the Qu'ran – the sacred scriptures; the Haddith – the actions and words of the Prophet Muhammed; and Shari'a law – the laws based on the Qu'ran. The result of the revolution was to turn Iran into a religious state.

Demonstration outside the American Embassy, Iran, during the Islamic Revolution of 1979.

In all these ways Islam was a radical force and without it the revolution would probably not have occurred. Contrary to the examples provided by Cohn (1970) and Adas (1979), where religious mobilization failed politically, such mobilization was successful in Iran. One other issue is important. On the face of it, Islam might appear to be a conservative force. For example, given that it requires a much higher level of religious activity than many other religions, it might be expected to inhibit the development of a modern capitalist society. That might be seen to be even more likely, given that Islamic law prohibits charging interest – what is called usury. Islam is also a religion which emphasizes the literal truth of the Qu'ran. However, Iran now has large-scale capitalist enterprises and a stock exchange involved in global share-trading and markets. Therefore, there seems to be no necessary link between Islam and a conservative attitude towards modernity. In reality, there are elements of what might appear to be conservatism in Islam – an emphasis on strong families, an opposition to adultery and to women wearing revealing clothing – but that does not seem to have inhibited the development of a complex modern society.

Essay question

On what basis does Marx describe religion as a conservative force and Weber describe it as potentially a force for social change? What evidence is there that either of them is correct?

Coursework suggestion

The development of capitalism – first in Britain, elsewhere in Europe, and the USA, and then on a global scale – is a fascinating subject for sociologists and historians. There are therefore many opportunities for interesting and innovative coursework. These could include investigating the religious history of your own neighbourhood in your local Public Records Office, or a detailed study of a religious movement that had a significant part in processes of social change – for example, Islam or Methodism.

References and further reading

Adas, M. (1979) *Prophets of Rebellion: Millenarian protest movements against European colonial order*, London: Cambridge University Press.

Cohn, N. (1970) *The Pursuit of the Millennium*, London: Paladin.

Halevy, E. (1924) *A History of the English People in 1815*, London: Unwin.

Halevy, E. (1927) *A History of the English People, 1830–1841*, London: Unwin.

Thompson, E.P. (1968) *The Making of the English Working Class*, Harmondsworth: Penguin.

Weber, M. (1904/1974) *The Protestant Ethic and the Spirit of Capitalism*, London: Unwin.

Worsley, P. (1968) *The Trumpet Shall Sound*, London: MacGibbon and Kee.

Religion and postmodernity

Introduction

This chapter examines the discussion within sociology about whether we now live in a **postmodern** society. Sociologists disagree about postmodernity – what it is and whether, indeed, it exists at all – and the extent to which it differs from modernity. The chapter goes on to ask what happens to religion in a postmodern society: for example, whether postmodernity leads to a resurgence of religious belief and practice, and therefore reverses the process of secularization discussed in Chapters 6 and 7.

Postmodernity: a general overview

The *post* in **postmodernity** is one clue to the meaning of the term and its relation to modernity: *postmodernity* comes *after* modernity. One of the defining characteristics of modernity (see Chapter 1, pp. 5–6) was a widespread belief in progress. Society's problems would eventually be solved by science and technology, which would help bring an end to such things as disease, inequality and poverty. Modern, efficient management in business and government would create jobs and wealth for all.

A great deal of philosophy and religion shared this kind of optimism. Marxism, for example, held that history would inevitably bring about a classless society, in which no one would be exploited. As a result, everyone would have the things they needed and find full expression for their talents and abilities. The Christian religions of Europe and North America were preached in the expanding empires of Britain and the other colonial powers. These religions also allied themselves with movements for social reform, so that optimism about the inevitability of social progress and the

Q: *What do you get if you cross a member of the Mafia with a postmodernist?*

A: *An offer you don't understand.*

onward march of humankind to a better future seemed justified by very real improvements in many people's lives; for example, those brought about by changes in public health policy and the development of modern medicine.

Postmodernism or postmodernity?

Generally, sociologists distinguish between *postmodernism* and *postmodernity*. Postmodernism is a label frequently used to describe a number of *cultural* features, such as the increasing significance of computers, the development of virtual realities, and new genres in fiction which de-emphasize narrative and plot. Postmodernity (or the postmodern society), on the other hand, refers to certain *structural* changes, such as globalization (see Chapter 5, pp. 57–8), the decline in class-based politics and the rise of environmental politics. Postmodernism is a consequence of *postmodernity*.

The collapse of the 'grand narrative'

In all these ways the belief in progress was allied to what are now known as **grand narratives**: overarching belief systems which claim universal legitimacy and authority. Religions such as Christianity and Islam, philosophies such as Marxism, and science in general all functioned as grand narratives: each of them claimed a superior status over all other belief systems; each of them claimed to describe the causes of social problems and inequalities; each of them held out the promise of a better future, whether it was religion's promise of salvation, Marxism's classless utopia or science's promise of material ease and plenty.

Over the last fifteen years or so, postmodernist theorists (first and foremost, Jean-François Lyotard) have described what they call the 'collapse of the grand narrative'. Science, technology and efficient management have lost much of their allure in a century which has witnessed two world wars of appalling devastation, the development of atomic and germ warfare, widening inequalities between rich and poor, and environmental destruction on a scale which threatens all life on earth. To many people, religions seem unable to account for such unprecedented evils. Perhaps the most recent and spectacular example of the collapse of a grand narrative is Marxism: the disintegration of the Soviet Union in 1989 discredited state Marxism by revealing widespread corruption and inefficiency.

Zygmunt Bauman (1997) argues that postmodernity necessarily involves this awareness of the failure of modernity:

> Postmodernity ... is the irretrievable loss of trust in the project of modernity and its ability to manage, enhance and ultimately to fulfil human potential ... [with] the prospect of living *without* security, guarantees and order.
>
> (Smart 1993, p. 102)

Symbols, signs and meanings

The collapse of the grand narrative is complemented by the effects of **globalization** on modern societies. Postmodernist theorists claim that globalization (see Chapter 5, pp. 57–8) has radically affected how we live our lives. Powerful communications technologies – predominantly television and computers – provide access to the cultures, ideas and products of the entire world, as a consequence of which local traditions can be threatened. We live in a world that is 'information rich', one in which there is an over-production of information, so that an enormous increase in cultural artefacts (for example, books, CDs, advertisements and 'clipart') from many different traditions can be studied and consumed. The interpretation of such information – the *meanings* we attach to the things we consume – is left more and more to the individual. In the language of the postmodernists, we *consume* the products, symbols and signs of a globalized economy, but we provide our *own* meanings and significance to these acts of consumption. According to Jean Baudrillard (1983, 1990), we are what we consume, and our identities are formed and changed through acts of consumption.

Signs of the times

Signs and symbols can take on a life of their own, irrespective of their original meanings. National flags can become objects of veneration in this way, even when their original purpose is forgotten or when the values for which they once stood are no longer accepted. Similarly, religious symbols can take on new meanings. One strand of Afro-Caribbean Rastafarianism in Britain, for example, involves styles of dress and the display of religious imagery, whose theological significance is sometimes forgotten. Also in Britain in recent years, some Christian churches de-emphasized their traditional symbol of the Cross: it could be argued that this was, in part, a recognition that postmodernity's proliferation of signs and symbols had drained the Cross of its significance.

We have already mentioned (Chapter 6, pp. 80–1) that one consequence of globalization for religions is that they become more like commodities: they compete to be consumed, or they remain unconsumed, just like any other commodity. The postmodernist extends this analysis by arguing that the signs and symbols of religion – the Islamic crescent moon, the Christian cross, for example – no longer have any stable, fixed meaning. Such signs and symbols have become appropriated by mass consumer culture, to be used and interpreted by consumers for their own – largely decorative and playful – purposes, such as jewellery.

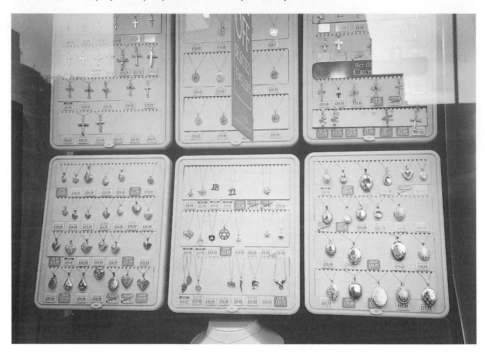

Inventing ourselves

Many of the signs and symbols, messages and images, which daily bombard individuals in a postmodern society are designed to sell a product or promote an organization. However, because there are so many of them, in many different media, postmodernists claim they have become 'free-floating', unattached from the things they are designed to help sell or promote. While postmodernists assert that we are more receptive than ever before to the messages of mass media, it is also the case that there are more messages than ever before, all of them competing for our attention. This encourages a 'pick and mix' culture in which individuals no longer identify with a single religion or political party for life. Instead, each of us experiments much more with creating his or her own identity: we select and blend our religious beliefs and practices, for example, from a variety of sources; we 'try them on for size' and discard them when they seem worn out. In doing all this we demonstrate that the individual self is much more 'fluid' than once thought: in the postmodernist world, our identities are no longer moulded by a unitary process of **socialization**; instead, we are constantly inventing our own selves.

Zygmunt Bauman (1997) claims that this consumption of goods and services becomes more and more important in people's lives as a way of constructing and changing identity; such consumption becomes a form of seduction, with advertising as allurement.

Many realities, no authorities

In addition to the enormous volume of media images to which we are exposed in a postmodernist society, there is also an emphasis on mixing styles and genres in such things as television programmes, films, architecture and literature. Politicians appear on comedy and game shows; the personal lives of religious leaders are held up to public scrutiny; religions and political systems are compared and criticized.

According to such thinkers as Baudrillard (1983, 1990), this characteristic of postmodernity makes it difficult (often impossible) to find reliable sources of authority that we can trust to guide us in our lives. Indeed, concepts such as authority and moral leadership are often undermined to such an extent that they no longer seem appropriate or relevant. In the past, we may have believed what we were told by religious leaders simply because they *were* religious leaders; this is no longer the case. Similarly, according to Jean-François Lyotard (1986), intellectuals cease to prescribe policies and courses of action and merely *interpret* events.

Politically, communities fragment, class-based political activity declines and – in the absence of clear moral and political rules – individual and group decisions about what to do and how to do it increase in significance. Politics and morality become more risky, unpredictable *and* also more important.

Another consequence is that it is very difficult (often impossible) to distinguish image from reality. According to Baudrillard (1983, 1990), the distinction between image

Postmodern architecture is eclectic: it mixes styles from different periods. The Ark, Hammersmith (top), the pyramid at the entrance to the Louvre, Paris.

and reality is itself ceasing to have any significance; instead, we live in a world of media simulations which are more real than the 'reality' we inhabit. The signs and symbols of postmodernity belong to **hyperreality**, by which Baudrillard means that they have no meaning beyond themselves: they refer only to themselves and not to an alleged 'reality'.

Baudrillard and the Gulf War

Jean Baudrillard's (1983, 1990) analysis of postmodernity is both complex and controversial. He stresses the importance of technology, in particular visual communications and computer technology: not only are there more things to communicate and faster ways of communicating them, but also we lose the ability to distinguish between images and the reality they represent; most of the time, we simply see the images.

After the Gulf War in 1992, Baudrillard published a book entitled *The Gulf War Did Not Take Place*. He pointed out that all that most people *thought* they knew about the Gulf War was contained in media presentations: they really only knew *images* of the Gulf War. For most people, therefore, there was no *real* Gulf War: it was fought on television. Baudrillard argues that television and computers create a totally new form of reality (what he calls **hyperreality**), so that what is alleged to be real (in this case, an event known as the Gulf War) is, in fact, no more real than the images presented on television. Even aircraft pilots who fought in the Gulf War experienced the combat via images on computer screens (for example, film transmitted by 'smart bombs' immediately before impact) and described it in terms of electronic computer games.

Summary

The sociological debate about postmodernity is a complex one. Different theorists of postmodernism – Baudrillard, Bauman and Lyotard, for example – have different emphases and interests. Postmodernism provides grounds for optimism and pessimism: on the one hand, its emphasis on plurality – involving the erosion of traditional social hierarchies and privileged sources of authority – can be seen as empowering for those groups formerly disempowered (among them, women, gays and ethnic minorities). On the other hand, its description of voracious globalized consumption can sound frighteningly chaotic.

In addition, postmodernity could perhaps be criticized for perpetuating the 'Western' bias of sociology (see Chapter 1, pp. 2–3). Many of the technological developments which appear crucial to theories of postmodernity (computers and television, for example, and media representations in general) are overwhelmingly consumed by the more affluent sectors of the most affluent societies. While postmodernists could claim that these specific features of postmodernity occur only in these sectors, it is important to remember that well over 50 per cent of the world's adult population has *never* used a telephone. Access to technology varies according to location and income; consequently, its effects on religions will also vary.

Anthony Giddens and late modernity

Giddens is an influential sociologist who claims that we live in a *late* modern – rather than a *post*modern – world. **Late modernity** is a new form of modernity that has not lost faith in what Giddens calls 'the project of modernity': the idea that progress and improvement are possible and likely. Society is now global and technologies of communication allow us to know about and try out many different cultures and ways of life. Society is *detraditionalized* (see pp. 171–2). In addition, because of the speed and global nature of communications, our very conceptions of space and time have changed – more and more things happen instantaneously. There is greater risk and uncertainty; risk is actually manufactured and created, and is no longer unexpected and unplanned. Risk emanates from a social system in which there is uncertainty, for example, about economic growth and the environment problems.

All the aspects of postmodernity discussed above reinforce one another so that – according to the postmodernists – we live in a society characterized by:

- the coexistence of many different subgroups and subcultures;
- the erosion of traditional social classes and class-based politics;
- the growth of movements such as environmentalism, feminism and ethnic politics;
- the diminished power of national governments to manage political and economic affairs;
- the rejection of cultural élitism;
- the absence of agreed standards for evaluating what is true or false, right or wrong, worthwhile or worthless;
- the blurring of the distinction between what is real and what is not;
- individual experimentation with self-identity by means of the consumption of culture – its products, beliefs and practices.

All of this has implications for religion and for the sociological study of religion. It is to these that we shall now turn.

Research and interpretation activity

Postmodernists emphasize the relativity of all claims to knowledge and authority. They also stress individualism and the emergence of new subcultures. What evidence is there in your locality (for example, the posters and noticeboards of places of worship) that religious organizations also recognize that society has changed in these ways? How have they responded?

Religion in a postmodern society

> Postmodernity has questioned the authorizing and legitimizing of both faith and reason, opting for the view that both offer stories of reality ... thus, although science and religion continue to spin their stories of things, they are increasingly doing so on the shifting sands of a postmodern outlook.
>
> (Natoli 1997, p. 15)

There are two important questions we can now ask:

● Are there aspects of religion today that are postmodern and which suggest that religion is just 'a story about society'?

● How far is religion a *response* to postmodernity; that is, to what extent do religions challenge the idea of a multiplicity of stories?

In thinking about these questions we will also reconsider some ideas about the secularization thesis discussed in Chapters 6 and 7.

Postmodern religions?

Chapter 5 discussed new religious movements (NRMs) and new age movements (NAMs) as examples of typical ways in which religiosity is now expressed. Are NRMs and NAMs types of religions that are typical of a postmodern world?

Welcome to the spiritual supermarket. Each person builds his or her own mosaic of practice, belief and experience. A lapsed Catholic described his fascination in Tibetan Buddhism, how his wife is on her local Church of England parish council, why he is delighted that his children are attending an Anglican primary school and how a Bon spiritual healer did wonders for his health (Bon is the Tibetan shamanistic religion that preceded the 9th century arrival of Buddhism). He rounded off this whistle-stop tour of spirituality – he had a lot of time for Hare Krishna and was complaining that he couldn't find tapes of Tibetan Buddhist chants – by admitting that he had baulked at being prescribed a deer's heart by his Bon healer.

In a recent report, the Church of England declared this kind of 'pick'n'mix' spirituality the greatest threat it faced. The report, Search for Faith, is a perceptive analysis of what customers are looking for in Britain's spiritual free market and how this is infiltrating and undermining orthodox Christianity. What it was far less confident about was what, if anything, the established Church could do about it. The enemy for believing Christians, it declared, is no longer secularism – does it exist? – but the fragmentation of belief and breaking down of boundaries between denominations, between faiths and between all spiritual beliefs.

Source: *The Guardian*, 16 December 1996

Hybridity

NRMs and NAMs are *hybrid*: they contain a mixture of several different traditions. The Unification Church, for example, is a combination of Hinduism, Buddhism and Christianity, and NAMs in general often contain mixtures of Christianity and older forms of religion, such as paganism.

This **hybridity** also seems to be part of the *appeal* of such religious movements. As with hybrid styles of cooking – meals that contain elements from English, French and Thai cuisine, for example – the appeal of such hybridity seems to be an essential feature of a postmodern society. The appeal of hybridity is linked to the postmodern emphasis on consumer choice and sophisticated marketing systems.

Part of the hybridity of many NRMs and NAMs involves an *ecumenical* view of beliefs themselves. The commitment to mixing different religious traditions suggests that **ecumenicalism** – a coming together of several religious traditions and the recognition that all such traditions have something to offer – is an important part of postmodern religion.

Research activity

Find two examples of hybrid new religious movements and two examples of hybrid new age movements. Which religious and other traditions do these movements draw on? If you have access to the Internet, you could try searching under new age.

Choice and consumption

Shopping is next to godliness

SOME PEOPLE love shopping, others hate it. But most seem to think it a subject unworthy of serious study.

For Daniel Miller, professor of anthropology at University College London, however, shopping is anything but frivolous. It is a highly responsible activity engaged in by responsible people showing concern for others. He knows because he has just carried out an ethnographic study of a street in North London, which involved accompanying people on everyday excursions to the supermarket.

Shopping, he says, does not simply reflect love but is a way in which love is expressed and reproduced. Take Mrs Wynn, a working-class housewife and childminder. She constantly monitors her family's preferences in order to satisfy them. But she also tries to change her loved ones. She forever wants them to eat healthier foods than they would choose for themselves. 'In short, her shopping is primarily an act of love, that in its daily conscientiousness becomes one of the primary means by which relationships of love and care are constituted in practice,' Miller writes.

Traditionally the people who grew crops and reared animals engaged in sacrifice before they consumed them, he explains. That created their relationship to the gods and their larger moral and religious values. Shopping performs the same function in our own society, Miller says. Like primitive humans, we do not wish simply to consume the things we have brought into being and nourished.

Just as people wanted to ensure that they gave to the gods through the ritual of sacrifice before they engaged in consumption, so we regard shopping as being about higher things – to do with nurturing social relations. 'I think we have other concerns and values,' he says. 'In the process of shopping we are expressing these other concerns. In that way it is like a religious activity for us.'

Source: *Times Higher Education Supplement*, 27 February 1998

As Bruce (1996) argues, modernity is characterized by individualism and the importance of individual choices about where to live, whom to marry, what to believe, and so on. However, in postmodernity there is not only a great deal more choice (as technologies make more and more things for people to consume), but also the act of choice itself becomes a central way in which people define their identities: 'I consume, therefore I am'.

Religion becomes part of this postmodern world of consumer choice; as we saw in Chapters 5 (pp. 65–7) and 7 (pp. 98–100), religious organizations market themselves. Many NRMs and NAMs make specific claims that if individuals choose them it will say a lot about the sort of people they are or are trying to become. There is, in this sense, a marketplace for religions in which religions compete with each other for consumers.

Research activity

Identify the major religious organizations in your locality. Look at their noticeboards and announcements. How far do these suggest that religion is a commodity that has to be marketed like any other commodity?

Spirituality

Heelas's (1996) study of the new age and Giddens's (1991) discussions of identity in the late modern world point to how new age beliefs in particular are concerned with spiritual issues in a wide range of everyday activities: work, diet, the environment, etc. For example, the idea that the environment is an organism which we can harm – the idea of Gaia (see Chapter 5, pp. 67–8) – can turn environmentalism into something very close to a religious movement. Satish Kumar puts forward this argument in favour of a spiritual view of the environment:

> The economy is booming and yet there is no 'feel good factor'. The supermarkets are full of food and yet people are spiritually starved. Highways are filled with high-speed cars but people feel they are getting nowhere … out of

A passion that is close to a religion?

a transformed [and spiritual] personal life social, political and ecological actions are also emerging. Meditation, veggie-box economies and climbing trees to stop road building are various dimensions of the same spiritual reality … in the spirit of dialogue there is no place for any kind of missionary zeal for the cause of spiritual ecology. There is no place for trying to convert people to a set dogma or creed. It is a matter of initiating conversations to find common ground among those who care for the earth and its people.

(Kumar 1997, p. 20)

Research and evaluation activity

Look at some publicity produced for the Body Shop. What picture of the natural environment does it present? To what extent could it be described as religious? How far does it correspond to Kumar's idea of a spiritual ecology?

One way of interpreting the role of spirituality in the new age is to see it as involving an attempt to *remystify* the world and to counter the processes of *demystification* originally identified by Max Weber (see Chapter 6, pp. 87–9).

Detraditionalization

Christianity lost in dome 'spirit zone'

THE CROSS, the 2,000-year-old symbol of Christianity has found no room in the Millennium Dome. Britain's established church is to play a secondary role in the celebrations at Greenwich, south London, because of the government's insistence on granting equal prominence to other religions.

A multi-faith exhibition, built around a giant glass tent, is to form the centrepiece of the dome's 'spirit zone'. It will display human rites of passage, religious rituals and images of devotional art.

Inside the Spiritual zone

Rites of passage

From birth to death, images of the achievements and reversals of 1,000 lives will create a modern version of the medieval wheel of life

Rituals in religion

In Jesus, God became man and in Christianity, as with every other religion, the rituals absorbed the natural rhythms of the lives of their devotees and the patterns of nature

Source: *The Sunday Times,* 14 June 1998

One aspect of late modernity which Giddens, especially, discusses is **detraditionalization**: the view that traditions lose their significance as more and more cultures and beliefs become available. Giddens claims that globalization (including global mass communications) tears traditions away from their points of origin.

Some aspects of NRMs and of the new age are indicative of this process. For example, the hybridity of many new religions implies that it does not really matter where a religious tradition originated because any religious tradition can work in almost any society. Religious traditions may simply have become a series of stories about how people live their lives, with no one story more or less correct than any other.

Along with this detraditionalization of religion, there is also a complete change of focus, described by Heelas as follows:

> *Autonomy* and *freedom* are highly valued; and *authority* lies with the *experience* of the *self* or, more broadly, the *natural realm*. This means that new agers attach great importance to the *self-ethic*, which includes emphasis on the exercise of *self-responsibility* ... detraditionalization is also associated with the movement's *perennialized* outlook, namely that the same wisdom can be found at the heart of all religious traditions.
>
> (Heelas 1996, p. 29)

In other words, detraditionalization is much more than an acceptance of the value of all traditions: it is also associated with a rejection of much of the underlying emphases of religious organization, for example on where authority resides. For NAMs, authority resides neither in tradition nor within a religious organization, but within the individual.

However, as we will see later (pp. 175–7), there are movements and forms of religious fundamentalism that counter the process of detraditionalization.

Self-orientation

Heelas's analysis of the new age makes it quite clear that the self is a central element in many new age beliefs and practices. The self as something we are encouraged to work upon and improve is also a feature of Giddens's discussions of late modernity. It is clear from our discussions in Chapters 5 and 7 that this concern with the self is also part of many NRMs: in Scientology, self-improvement is a central aim and a promise made to followers (see Chapter 5, pp. 60–4).

This orientation toward the self varies between NRMs and NAMs. NRMs tend to view the self as something that has to be mastered and changed in order for a person to improve in their job, relationship, and so on. This is the aim of Exegesis seminars (see Chapter 5, pp. 70–1), where the old self is abandoned and a new, more effective self is taken on. In NAMs the self is more spiritual, with less emphasis on self-mastery and finding a new self in order to achieve practical aims. Instead, emphasis is placed much more on self-realization.

Religion and communications technology

We saw in Chapter 7 (pp. 98–100) the extent to which a wide range of religious movements – mainstream and new – use mass communications technologies to disseminate their ideas. However, many NRMs and NAMs use advanced communications technologies much more radically: for example, many have their own websites and thus the potential for a very dispersed membership, which can be in contact at any time and anywhere in the world. This is, of course, one of the factors that tear religions from their original social locations and lead to detraditionalization.

Through a glass, brightly: the Church goes online

In the long parade of schism, dispute and persecution which is so great a part in Church history, there can rarely have been as heartrending a moment as the recent scene when one vicar asked: 'Have you any room for a Mac user?' It was if the eye of the needle were an open gate by comparison with The Church Computer Users' Group, one of many organisations to have a stand at the Christian Resources Exhibition in a converted railway station in Manchester.

The Rev Paul Knight, the Right Rev Colin Scott and the Rev Jason Boyd surf the Net at the Christian Resources Exhibition.

Source: *The Daily Telegraph*, 18 November 1997

The use of advanced computer technology may also make possible postmodern, virtual religions. Chapter **7** (pp. 98–100) discussed the importance of television to religion in the USA. However, the use of advanced technology is much more widespread and has the potential to extend the scope of detraditionalization and consumer choice, to the extent that religions could even exist *solely* on the Internet.

Research activity

If you have access to the Internet, try to find examples of religious organizations that have websites. Do these include both mainstream religions and new age movements? Examine how and what these websites communicate. Do your findings suggest that these are now postmodern religions?

Religious organizations as postmodern organizations

Stewart Clegg (1992) discusses the development of postmodern organizations in Japanese industry and identifies a number of key features that contrast with those of organizations characteristic of modernity (see Table 11.1).

Table 11.1 Modern versus postmodern organizations

Modern organizations	Postmodern organizations
Rigid, with authoritarian control	Flexible, with democratic control
Focused on mass consumption	Focused on niche markets
Dominated by technology	Enabled by technology
Demarcated and deskilled jobs	Undemarcated and multi-skilled jobs

The types of religious organization typical of modernity – churches, sects – are very similar to the *modern* industrial organizations described by Clegg. They are hierarchical, with clear job demarcations, and they focus on 'mass consumption' in their attempts to recruit as many people as possible with the same message. They do not, however, generally use any particular modern technology.

NAMs are much more like the *postmodern* industrial organizations, which Clegg regards as characteristic of Japanese industry. They are often democratic rather than rigid and authoritarian. They focus on niche markets and rarely try to recruit as many members as churches try to recruit. NAMs take the same positive attitude to communications technologies as many industrial corporations. They view members as possessing the flexibility and adaptability that industrial corporations wish to encourage in their employees; indeed, their focus on self-improvement and self-mastery is exactly the sort of 'work' discipline that industrialists demand. It is this latter feature of 'self-religions' (see Chapter 5, pp. 63 and 68) that leads Heelas (1992) to describe many NAMs as 'cults for capitalism'.

Research and interpretation activity

What evidence is there for and against the argument that aspects of new religious movements and the new age are examples of postmodern *religions?*

For	Against

Log on, all ye faithful

LOOKING to live up to the proclamations of business experts, who have declared that Christmas online shopping will cross over to the mainstream (at least in the US), Net retailers seem to be going all out to exploit the seasonal spirit.

However, there are those who argue that the Net can actually offer something more profound. It can help you leave behind money-grabbing profanity and deliver a real sense of spiritual connection.

This isn't just a matter of established religious faiths using the Net to spread their particular word. Rather, for some, the Net seems to have become an object of devotion and reverence. These online seekers don't log on looking for ways to get the kids that Christmas present Furby. They start up their browsers in search of spiritual renewal.

Spirits of the Web

The Noosphere
www.technoetic.com/
noosphere/index.html
Inspired by the writings of Teilhard de Chardin

The Church of Virus
www.lucifer.com/virus/
A kind of evolutionary belief system. The site features lists of Virian virtues and sins (reason is good, dogma bad) and claims Charles Darwin as the first Virian Saint.

Technosophy
www.technosophy.com
Leading off with Arthur C Clarke's old saw 'any sufficiently advanced technology is indistinguishable from magic', this aims to show that 'everything in Nature, including the Universe, is technologically organised'.

Chaos Magick
www.fused.com/trap14/
A techno-pagan site – how to use 'magick techniques' for online collective rituals.

According to the American writer Erik Davis, cybertheology is just one example from a long history of attempts to project spiritual hopes and fears onto technology. In Techgnosis, he sets out a kind of secret history of the way mystical visions and dreams have always clustered around new technology, in particular communications technology.

Davis points out that religious images have always filled writings about the Net. For example, in William Gibson's cyberpunk sci-fi novel Neuromancer, the Net is inhabited by artificial intelligence that at the end of the book achieves something like godhead. In subsequent books, cyberspace is presented as a place haunted by various gods.

Source: *The Guardian*, 10 December 1998

Fundamentalism: a response to postmodernity?

Chapter 7 (pp. 98–101) discussed the role of the Christian Right in the USA and the increasing significance of forms of religious and political fundamentalism. We can now ask:

● how far are these phenomena responses to postmodernity, in particular to the postmodern emphasis on choice, relativism, the end of traditions and hybridity?

Both Bauman and Giddens think that fundamentalism is a response to postmodernity/late modernity. Giddens thinks that the major problem with late modernity centres on issues of doubt and risk:

[Late modernity is] a system in which areas of relative security interlace with radical doubt and with disquieting scenarios of risk … it is easy to see why religious fundamentalism has a special appeal.

(Giddens 1991, p. 207)

Giddens, A. (1990) *Consequences of Modernity*, Cambridge: Polity Press.
Giddens, A. (1991) *Modernity and Self Identity*, Cambridge: Polity Press.
Heelas, P. (1992) 'The sacralization of the self and new age capitalism', in N. Abercrombie and A. Warde (eds), *Social Change in Contemporary Britain*, Cambridge: Polity Press, pp. 136–66.
Heelas, P. (1996) *The New Age Movement*, Cambridge: Polity Press.
Kumar, S. (1997), 'Green Spirit', in *Keeping the Faiths: the new covenant between religious belief and secular power, Demos*, No. 11, pp. 18–20.
Lyotard, J.-F. (1986) *The Postmodern Condition*, Manchester: Manchester University Press.
Mills, C.W. (1970) *The Sociological Imagination*, Harmondsworth: Penguin.
Natoli, J. (1997) *A Primer to Postmodernity*, Oxford: Blackwell Publishers.
Smart, B. (1993) *Postmodernity*, London: Routledge.

Appendix

What do sociologists find interesting about some selected world religions?

Founded in about the twentieth century BCE.

Judaism

- The role that Judaism plays in politics.
- The importance of Jewish orthodoxy.
- The analysis of the effects of the holocaust and other persecutions and the historical role of anti-Semitism.
- The importance of religious books and how they are interpreted.

Founded in about the fourteenth century BCE in India.

Hinduism

- The importance of polytheism (many gods).
- The relationships between religion and the caste system.
- The significance of religious festivals.
- The importance of religious books and how they are interpreted.

Founded in the sixth century BCE in China.

Confucianism

- Confucianism as a religion without some of the essential features of religion: it has no clergy, no gods, and there is no belief in life after death.
- Confucianism as a system of ethics: that is, about how people should live their lives.
- The importance of self control.
- The importance of ritual and of tradition.

Founded in the sixth century BCE in China.

Taoism

- The role that magic plays in religious belief and practice.
- The close relationships between society and the natural order and environment.
- The importance of meditation.
- The importance of following religious rituals.

Buddhism

- The role that Buddhism plays in adjusting to the reality of the world.
- The importance of monasticism.
- The importance of strict discipline in attaining salvation.
- The appeal of Buddhism in late modern societies.

Founded in the fifth century BCE in India.

Christianity

- The importance of charisma (Jesus Christ).
- The movement from sect to church.
- The role of sects in Christianity.
- The role of Christianity as a state religion.
- The importance of monotheism (one God).
- The development of denominations.
- The relationships between the message of Christianity – loving thy neighbour – and its role in some major social and political conflicts.

Founded in the first century CE in what is now Israel.

Islam

- The close links between Islam and Christianity in terms of belief.
- The relationship between Islam and the growth of a modern, capitalist society.
- The role that suffering plays in religious salvation.
- The relationship between religion and politics.
- The fear of Islam and the negative stereotyping of Islamic fundamentalism.
- The role of women in Islam.
- How a belief in the importance of suffering can turn inwards, physical self-punishment, or outwards, punishment of those who do not believe.

Founded in Medina, Saudi Arabia, in the seventh century CE.

Sikhism

- The importance in Sikhism of religious teachers rather than gods.
- The absence of priests.
- The importance of meditation.

Founded in the fifteenth century CE in India.

Bibliography

Adas, M. (1979) *Prophets of Rebellion: Millenarian protest movements against European colonial order*, London: Cambridge University Press.

Anderson, B. (1983) *Imagined Communities*, London: Verso.

Anwar, M. (1981) *Between Two Cultures: A study of relationships between generations in the Asian community in Britain*, London: Commission for Racial Equality.

Ash, R. and Goodchild, I. (1997) 'Poles apart – secularisation and Anglo-Jewry', *Sociology Review*, 7:1, pp. 9–13.

Barker, E. (1984) *The Making of a Moonie*, Oxford: Blackwell.

Barker, E., Halman, L. and Vloet, A. (1993) *The European Values Study, 1981–1990, Summary Report*, London/Netherlands: EVS Group.

Barrett, L. (1977) *The Rastafarians: The dreadlocks of Jamaica*, Kingston (Jamaica): Sangster Books.

Baudrillard, J. (1983) *Simulations*, New York: Semiotexte.

Baudrillard, J. (1990) *Fatal Strategies*, New York: Semiotexte.

Bauman, Z. (1992) *Intimations of Postmodernity*, London: Routledge.

Bauman, Z. (1997) *Postmodernity and its Discontents*, Cambridge: Polity Press.

Beck, U. (1992) *Risk Society*, London: Sage.

Becker, E. (1932) *Systematic Sociology*, New York: John Wiley.

Beckford, J. (1996) 'Postmodernity, high modernity and new modernity: three concepts in search of religion', in K. Flanagan and P. Jupp, *Postmodernity, Sociology and Religion*, London: Macmillan/St Martin's Press.

Bellah, R. (1970) 'Civil religion in America', in *Beyond Belief: Essays in religion in a post-traditional world*, pp. 168–89, New York: Harper and Row.

Bellah, R. (1975) *The Broken Covenant: American civil religion in a time of trial*, New York: Seabury Press.

Berger, P. (1973) *The Social Reality of Religion*, Harmondsworth: Penguin.

Beyer, P. (1994) *Religion and Globalization*, London: Sage.

Bibby, R. (1974) 'Sources of religious involvement', *Review of Religious Research*, 15:71–9.

Bibby, R. (1990) *Fragmented Gods*, Toronto: Stoddart.

Boal, F. (1982) 'Segregating and mixing: space and residence in Belfast', in F. Boal and J. Douglas (eds), *Integration and Division*, pp. 249–80, London: Academic Press.

Bocock, R. and Thompson, K. (1985) *Religion and Ideology*, Manchester: Manchester University Press and Open University.

Brierley, P. (1991) *Christian England*, London: Marc Europe.

Brierley, P. and Hiscock, V. (1993) *UK Christian Handbook*, London: Christian Research Association.

Brook, I. (1992) *British Social Attitudes: Cumulative source book, the first six surveys*, London: Gower.

Bruce, S. (1986) *God Save Ulster: The religion and politics of Paisleyism*, Oxford: Oxford University Press.

Bruce, S. (1990) *Pray TV: Televangelism in America*, London: Routledge.

Bruce, S. (1995) *Religion in Modern Britain*, Oxford: Oxford University Press.

Bruce, S. (1996) *Religion in the Modern World: From cathedrals to cults*, Oxford: Oxford University Press.

Butler, C. (1995) 'Religion and gender: young Muslim women in Britain', *Sociology Review*, 4:2, pp. 18–22.

Campbell, C. (1972) 'The cult, the cultic milieu and secularisation', in M. Hill (ed.), *A Sociological Yearbook of Religion*, No. 5, pp. 119–36, London: SCM Press.

Chaney, D. (1983) 'The symbolic mirror of ourselves: civic ritual in mass society' *Media, Culture and Society*, 5.2, pp. 119–35.

Clegg, S. (1992) 'Modern and postmodern organizations', *Sociology Review*, 1:4, pp. 24–8.

Cohn, N. (1970) *The Pursuit of the Millennium*, London: Paladin.

Coles, R. (1975) 'Football as "surrogate" religion', in M. Hill (ed.), *A Sociological Yearbook of Religion*, pp. 61–77, London: SCM Press.

Davie, G. (1990a) 'Believing without belonging: is this the future of religion in Britain?', *Social Compass*, 37:4, pp. 451–69.

Davie, G. (1990b) 'An ordinary God: the paradox of religion in contemporary Britain', *British Journal of Sociology*, 41:3, pp. 395–421.

Davie, G. (1994) *Religion in Britain since 1945: Believing without belonging*, Oxford: Blackwell.

Davie, G. (1995) 'Competing fundamentalisms', *Sociology Review*, 4:4, pp. 2–7.

Davie, G. (1997) 'The individualisation of British belief', in *Keeping the Faith*, Demos, no. 11, pp. 11–14.

Douglas, M. (1966) *Purity and Prayer*, London: Routledge.

Durkheim, E. (1912/1961) *The Elementary Forms of the Religious Life*, London: Allen and Unwin.

Elias, N. and Dunning, E. (1993) *The Quest for Excitement: Sport and leisure in the civilising process*, Oxford: Blackwell.

Evans-Pritchard, E.E. (1965) *Theories of Primitive Religion*, Oxford: Clarendon Press.

Flanagan, K. and Jupp, P. (1996) *Postmodernity, Sociology and Religion*, London: Macmillan/St Martin's Press.

Freud, S. (1927/1985) 'The Future of an Illusion', in *Civilisation, Society and Religion*, The Pelican Freud Library, vol. 12, Harmondsworth: Penguin.

Geertz, C. (1966) 'Religion as a cultural system', in M. Banton (ed.), *Anthropological Approaches to the Study of Religion*, pp. 1–44, ASA Monograph 3, London: Tavistock Publications.

Gerth, H. and Mills, C.W. (1948) *From Max Weber: Essays in Sociology*, London, Routledge.

Giddens, A. (1990) *Consequences of Modernity*, Cambridge: Polity Press.

Giddens, A. (1991) *Modernity and Self Identity*, Cambridge: Polity Press.

Glock, Y. and Stark, R. (1965) *Religion and Society in Tension*, New York: Rand McNally.

Gluckman, M. (1956) *Custom and Conflict in Africa*, Oxford: Blackwell.

Greeley, A. (1982) *Religion: A Secular Theory*, New York: Free Press.

Halevy, E. (1924) *A History of the English People in 1815*, London: Unwin.

Halevy, E. (1927) *A History of the English People, 1830–1841*, London: Unwin.

Hall, S. (1985) 'Religious ideologies and social movements in Jamaica', in R. Bocock and K. Thompson, *Religion and Ideology*, pp. 269–96, Manchester: Manchester University Press and Open University.

Hamilton, M.B. (1995) *The Sociology of Religion*, London: Routledge.

Hamilton, M. (1998) 'Secularisation: now you see it, now you don't', *Sociology Review*, 7:4, pp. 27–31.

Hawley, J.S. (1994) *Fundamentalism and Gender*, Oxford: Oxford University Press.

Heelas, P. (1992) 'The sacralization of the self and new age capitalism', in N. Abercrombie and A. Warde (eds), *Social Change in Contemporary Britain*, pp. 136–66, Cambridge: Polity Press.

Heelas, P. (1996) *The New Age Movement*, Cambridge: Polity Press.

Helle, H. and Nieder, L. (1997) *Essay of Religion: Georg Simmel*, London: Yale University Press.

Herberg, W. (1983) *Protestant, Catholic and Jew: An essay in American Religious Sociology*, New York: Doubleday.

Hill, M. (1973) *A Sociology of Religion*, London: Heinemann.

Hinnells, J. (1997) *The New Handbook of Living Religions*, London: Blackwell.

Hobsbawm, E. (1959) *Primitive Rebels*, Manchester: Manchester University Press.

Holm, T. and Bowker, J. (1994) *Women in Religion*, London: Pinter Publishers.

Jacobs, E. and Worcester, R. (1994) *Britain under the MORI-scope*, London: Wiedenfeld and Nicholson.

James, W. (1971) *The Varieties of Religious Experience*, London: HarperCollins Publishers.

Jarman, N. (1997) *Material Conflicts: Parades and visual display in Northern Ireland*, Oxford: Berg.

Jenkins, R. (1997) *Rethinking Ethnicity*, London: Sage.

Johal, S. (1998) 'Brimful of Brasia', *Sociology Review*, 8:1, pp. 5–8

Johnson, A.G. (1995) *A Blackwell Dictionary of Sociology*, Oxford: Blackwell.

King, U. (1987) *Women in the World's Religions: past and present*, New York: Paragon House.

Kumar, S. (1997) 'Green Spirit' in *Keeping the Faith: The new covenant between religious belief and secular power*, Demos, No. 11, pp. 18–20.

Lane, C. (1981) *Rites of Rulers: Ritual in industrial society, the Soviet case*, Cambridge: Cambridge University Press.

Lasch, C. (1991) *The Culture of Narcissism*, New York: W.W.Norton & Company Ltd.

Lyotard, J.-F. (1986) *The Postmodern Condition*, Manchester: Manchester University Press.

Malinowski, B. (1922) *Argonauts of the Western Pacific*, London: Routledge and Kegan Paul.

Martin, D. (1967) *The Sociology of English Religion*, London: Routledge.

Martin, D. (1969) *The Religious and the Secular*, London: Heinemann.

Martin, D. (1996) 'Religion, secularisation and post-modernity', in P. Repstad (ed.), *Religion and Modernity: Modes of co-existence*, pp. 35–44, Oslo: Scandinavian Universities Press.

Marx, K. and Engels, F. (1845/1955) *On Religion*, Moscow: Progress Publishers.

Merton, R.K. (1957) *Social Theory and Social Structure*, Glencoe: Free Press.

Mills, C.W. (1970) *The Sociological Imagination*, Harmondsworth: Penguin.

Modood, T. and Berthoud, R. *et al* (1997) *Ethnic Minorities in Britain: Diversity and disadvantage*, The Fourth National Survey of Ethnic Minorities, London: Policy Studies Institute.

Natoli, J. (1997) *A Primer to Postmodernity*, Oxford: Blackwell Publishers.

Niebuhr, H.R. (1962) *The Social Sources of Denominationalism*, New York: Meridian.

ONS (1993) *1991 Census: Ethnic Group and Country of Birth*, London: Office for National Statistics.

Parsons, T. (1951) *The Social System*, New York: Basic Books.

Peach, C. (1996) 'Ethnicity in the 1991 Census', *The Ethnic Minority Populations of Great Britain*, Vol. 2, London: HMSO.

Pickering, W.S.F. (1984) *Durkheim's Sociology of Religion*, London: Routledge.

Pilkington, A. (1995) 'Globalisation and cultural identity', *Social Science Teacher*, 25:1, pp. 12–16.

Pryce, K. (1979) *Endless Pressure: A study of West Indian lifestyles in Bristol*, Harmondsworth: Penguin.

Puttick, K. (1997) *Women in New Religions: In search of community, sexuality and spiritual power*, London: Sage.

Repstad, P. (1996) *Religion and Modernity: Modes of co-existence*, Oslo: Scandinavian Universities Press.

Radcliffe-Brown, E. (1952) 'Religion and society', in *Structure and Function in Primitive Society*, pp. 153–77, London: Cohen and West.

Runciman, W.G. (1978) *Max Weber: Selections in translation*, Cambridge: Cambridge University Press.

Said, E. (1985) *Orientalism*, Harmondsworth: Penguin.

Sharma, A. (1987) *Women in World Religion*, Albany (US): State University of New York Press.

Shils, E. and Young, M. (1953) 'The meaning of the Coronation', *Sociological Review*, 1:2, pp. 63–82.

Shiner, L. (1967) 'The concept of secularisation in empirical research', *Journal of the Scientific Study of Religion*, Vol. 6, pp. 207–20.

Showalter, E. (1997) *Hystories: Hysteria, Gender and Culture*, London: Picador.

Simmel, G. (1898/1997) *Essays of Religion*, H. Helle and L. Nierder (eds), London: Yale University Press.

Smart, B. (1993) *Postmodernity* London: Routledge.

Stark, R. and Bainbridge, W. (1985) *The Future of Religion: Secularisation, revival and cult formation*, Berkeley: University of California Press.

Thomas, K. (1973) *Religion and the Decline of Magic*, Harmondsworth: Penguin.

Thompson, D. (1996) *The End of Time: Faith and fear in the shadow of the millennium*, London: Sinclair Stevenson.

Thompson, E.P. (1968) *The Making of the English Working Class*, Harmondsworth: Penguin.

Troeltsch, E. (1931/1976) *The Social Teachings of the Christian Churches*, Chicago: University of Chicago Press.

Turner, B. (1983) *Religion and Social Theory*, London: Sage.

Walby, S. (1992) *Theorising Patriarchy*, Oxford: Blackwell.

Walker, A. (1990) 'Why are most churchgoers women?', *Vox Angelica*, 20, pp. 73–90.

Wallis, R. (1976) *The Road to Total Suspicion: A sociological analysis of Scientology*, London: Heinemann.

Wallis, R. (1984) *The Elementary Forms of the New Religious Life*, London: Routledge.

Wallis, R. (1993) 'Charisma and explanation', in E. Barker, J. Beckford and K. Dobbelaere (eds), *Secularization, Rationalism and Sectarianism: Essays in honour of Bryan R Wilson*, pp. 167–80, Oxford: Clarendon Press.

Waters, M. (1995) *Globalization*, London: Routledge.

Watson, H. (1994) 'Women and the veil: personal responses to global process', in A.S. Ahmed and H. Donnan, *Islam, globalization and postmodernity*, pp. 141–59, London: Routledge.

Weber, M. (1904 /1974) *The Protestant Ethic and the Spirit of Capitalism*, London: Unwin.

Weber, M. (1922/1968) *Economy and Society*, Berkeley: University of California Press.

Weber, M. (1919 /1970) 'Politics as a vocation', in H. Gerth and C.W. Mills, (1948) *From Max Weber: Essays in Sociology*, pp. 77–128, London: Routledge.

Weber, M. (1922a/1978) 'The social psychology of the world religions', in H. Gerth and C.W. Mills, (1948) *From Max Weber: Essays in Sociology*, pp. 267–301, London: Routledge.

Weber, M. (1922b/1978) 'The soteriology of the underprivileged', in W.G. Runciman, *Max Weber: Selections in translation*, pp. 174–9, Cambridge: Cambridge University Press.

Wilson, B. (1961) *Sects and Society*, London: Heinemann.

Wilson, B. (1966) *Religion in Secular Society*, London: Watts.

Wilson, B. (1975) *The Noble Savages: The primitive origins of charisma and its contemporary survival*, Berkeley: University of California Press.

Wilson, B. (1982) *Religion in Sociological Perspective*, London: Oxford University Press.

Wilson, B. (1988) 'Secularisation: religion in the modern world', in S. Sutherland and P. Clarke (eds), *The World's Religions: The study of religion, traditional and new religions*, pp. 195–208, London: Routledge.

Winter, M. and Short, C. (1993) 'Believing and belonging: religion in rural England'. *British Journal of Sociology*, 44:4, pp. 635–51.

Wolff, K.H. (1964) *The Sociology of Georg Simmel*, New York: Free Press.

Worsley, P. (1968) *The Trumpet Shall Sound*, London: MacGibbon and Kee.

Yinger, J.M. (1957) *Religion, Society and the Individual: An introduction to the sociology of religion*, New York: Macmillan.

Index